P9-BBQ-857

# IMAGES OF LUNENBURG COUNTY

# IMAGES OF LUNENBURG COUNTY

**Photographs by Peter Barss**

Text recorded and edited by Peter Barss

Transcription by Myra and Peter Barss

**McClelland and Stewart**

McClelland and
Stewart Limited,
25 Hollinger Road,
Toronto, Ontario.
M4B 3G2

Designed by
David Perry

Printed and bound
in Canada

CANADIAN CATALOGUING IN PUBLICATION DATA

Barss, Peter, 1941-
Images of Lunenburg County

ISBN 0-7710-1087-7

1. Fishermen – Nova Scotia – Lunenburg County – Interviews 2. Lunenburg, N.S. (County) – History. I. Title.

SH224.N8B37 639'.22'0971623 C78-001453-7

For Ingram and Patchen

# Foreword

The first impression most people receive when they look at the work of Peter Barss is his delightful rapport with his subjects. You sense it immediately in his photographs where you realize he has their complete trust and they can forget themselves as they concentrate on their topic of conversation. It is evident too in their interviews when you know at once that their stories are authentic and not exaggerated to impress a new listener. His fishermen lived hard lives and were courageous beyond belief, and all for so little financial return. In these days it seems incredible. Yet they were fine God-fearing people, highly respected in their community, and deservedly so.

We can be grateful that this fast disappearing mode of life in Lunenburg County has been preserved in the excellent form presented here. Having interviewed so many such informants myself, it is with pride and pleasure that I commend this book for your perusal.

*Helen Creighton*

# Preface

For generations, young men along the coast of Nova Scotia have followed their fathers to sea. In 1972, when I first started to document what remains of this tradition in Lunenburg County, a fisherman in his seventies, Sydney Tanner, told me that he was glad to let me tape stories of his experiences at sea because otherwise, "When us old fellers are gone the younger people won't know what it was like." Sydney Tanner died in November, 1975.

Mr. Tanner was referring to the days of schooner fishing symbolized by the launching in 1921 of the legendary *Bluenose* in the town of Lunenburg. We too easily romanticize those days. Men and young boys sailed for the fishing grounds knowing they would have little or no contact with their families during the three month trip. The women were left behind to rear the children, grow gardens, and care for animals. Hundreds of men never returned: all too frequently men fishing a few miles from the vessel in their small dories were lost without a trace, and it was not uncommon for a vessel to go down with all hands in a storm. News of a man or a ship missing at sea often did not reach home for weeks after the tragedy. A man might return to find that his child, father or close friend had died in his absence. The work was hard and the shares the men earned on the vessels allowed them to survive but not much more. However, life was not all hardship and the poverty that existed was only economic and did not determine the quality of life. Villages were communities of people who shared hard times and joyful times. "In them days people was poorer . . . but they was happier."

Communities were isolated. One man from the LaHave Islands recalled the time when families travelled by horse and cart to Bridgewater – fifteen miles away – once a year to buy staple provisions. Because of this isolation, communities were nearly self-sufficient; families were closer and people depended on each other for survival – and for entertainment. When a family needed wood for the winter, men from the community turned out early in the morning for a sawing party. And while the men cut wood, the women worked together on a quilt. At night men and women came together for a dance in a "store" or fish shed. That was before television or cars.

Like Sydney Tanner, those days are gone forever. Some of the spirit, however, remains in the lives of the shore fishermen of today who, in the main, either sailed on the schooners themselves or are the sons of vessel fishermen. The human values that grow out of tightly knit families and communities – honesty, kindness, respect for others, a willingness to share – are not empty *clichés* to these men but are intrinsic parts of their lives. Perhaps the humility that generates these values comes from making a living from the sea and having to deal with the awesome forces of the elements which urge a man to sense his own fragility in the scheme of things.

But progress is taking its toll. Off-shore draggers destroy thousands of young fish daily and at the same time tear up the bottom – destroying spawning and feeding grounds. In-shore fish become scarcer and scarcer. Bureaucrats set quotas and, in order to avoid penalties, draggers dump tons of dead haddock and other fish overboard. A two hundred mile limit has been delineated on maps with the promise that fish stocks will replenish themselves. But while the bureaucrats talk to each other, mulling over statistics and graphs, the fishermen talk to their sons, "I ain't fussy 'bout you fishin'. In five, six years – maybe less – there ain't goin' to be no fish to get." And the young men leave for the factories, the offices, the cities.

Within the memories of some of the older men interviewed for this book, the villages of Lunenburg County sent one of the world's largest and most respected fishing fleets to The Grand Banks. These villages, once vibrant with activity, are now in a period of quiet transition. Each year there are fewer young men fishing beside their fathers, and as their tradition dies so does a way of life. No one I spoke to wanted to "turn the clock back," yet everyone expressed a sense of loss. Indeed, something is lost here, not just for the fishermen but for all of us. Their lives are a testament to individual human dignity and strength, qualities which are easily submerged by our modern society. These men are talking to us and we should listen; their experience speaks to the human condition.

The text moves in time from the vessel fishing days to the present. The photographs record what is left.

*P.B.*

# A Note on the Text

Material for this book was collected in sixty-two interviews with fishermen. The editing process was primarily one of elimination: stories that lacked interest, or that were repetitious, as well as digressions within usable stories were deleted from the 1,500 pages of original transcription. In a very few cases, where the opinions or feelings of two or three speakers coincided, I felt justified in combining those statements. For example, if one fisherman expressed doubt about the future of in-shore fishing because of the draggers and another mentioned the high cost of gear as a factor, I felt it fair to use both ideas as one statement. In no case was the wording, syntax, or substance of any passage altered from what was given to me on tape.

My intent has been to include stories that are of interest in and of themselves and that, when combined, constitute a more inclusive portrayal of the fishermen. It is their story in their words. I have arranged the stories in loose chronological order and according to theme.

In the interest of accuracy, I visited all the men I interviewed after the material was transcribed to check the names of crew members, Captains, vessels, and places. In addition to this very concrete information, there were a number of phrases that were impossible to understand on the tapes. I doubted that the men would recall these phrases, most of which were not particularly important to the story as a whole. After I read the preceding line or two, most of the men not only recalled the missing phrase but continued telling the story from that point on in words almost identical to those I had recorded over a year before. These stories are part of a rapidly disappearing oral tradition.

*P.B.*

Oh we'll heave up our anchor
Along our lee bow
Hooray fare ye well
Goodbye fare you well
Oh heave up our anchor
Along our lee bow
Hooray my boys for home
We're bound homeward bound
For Lunenburg town
Hooray fare you well
Goodbye fare you well
Homeward bound
For Lunenburg town
Hooray my boys hooray
Oh set our big mainsail
Along our broad stern
Hooray fare you well
Goodbye fare you well
Oh set our big mainsail
Along our broad stern
Hooray my boys
We're homeward bound
Oh set our gaff topsail
Along our top mast
Hooray fare you well
Goodbye fare you well
Oh set our gaff topsail
Along our top mast
Hooray my boys
We're homeward bound
Homeward bound
For Lunenburg town
Hooray fare you well
Goodbye fare you well
Homeward bound
For Lunenburg town
Hooray my boys hooray.

We used to sing that on the vessel heavin' up the anchor . . . y'know, when the vessel was loaded wit' fish an' the trip was done – when we was gettin' ready for to come home off o' The Banks. Heavin' up the anchor, you know – our side best, our side best. Headin' for in . . . .

– *Samuel Whynacht, second hand,* Bluenose I

# Them Big White Sails

# A Boy is Only a Boy

Through here – Mahone Bay, Lunenburg, Riverport, we had a hundred an' sixty-two fishin' vessels. That's some fishin' vessels. Why you go to Lunenburg an' get up on one end o' the wharves there an' look down o'er, well it was the same as woods. Spars looked like a forest, you. The harbours layed full o' vessels – three masters an' four masters – fishin' vessels. An' today there's none. It was somethin' pretty to see. And the vessels would leave for out in the spring o' the year . . . after the men that went had their plantin' done. Got the gardens all in before they went down on the trip, you. An' in the spring time, when we'd go away, you know, on what you call a frozen baitin' – the wind would be died out an' here'd be all those vessels goin' out with their flags flyin' – just enough wind to keep the flag out. I can see them big white sails yet.

Yes it was a pretty sight . . . 'course was a lot o' men that went out o' these harbours an' never come back too. Their bones are layin' down there yet.

Now when we went vessel fishin' we always had boys, y'know, two boys or three. Boys maybe ten, eleven, twelve year old. The youngest was most generally what you call flunky or catchy – same t'ing. An' the little flunky, he cut the tongues out, tongues an' cheeks. He'd cut 'em out an' put 'em in a big pork barrel – one o' them great big barrels . . . two hundred pounds. Salt 'em down in that. An' then he used to get . . . I don't know what it was. It wasn't very much – eight or nine cents or somethin' a pound. Somethin' like that. An' a lot o' tongues was in a barrel, I want'a tell you – salt shrinks 'em up, you understand. An' they'd have a header an' t'roater. An' the header – one feller takin' the heads off o' the fish. An' the t'roater – he would t'roat 'em an' gut. They was paid so much wages, see. They'd go on that till they learnt to go in a dory an' fish off the vessel.

An' some o' them old fellers used to go an' treat 'em hard, I'll tell you. A lot o' work . . . to fork them big fish along the deck an' put 'em in . . . they had to fork 'em three times to get 'em in the ked. That was hard work . . . t'inkin' about home an' everyt'ing.

When I was cook, I could help 'em out a little . . . I was always good to 'em. I always used to help 'em out forkin' the fish . . . you know a boy is only a boy.

I went on my first vessel to The Banks in 1912. Two years after Halley's comet went by here. Went right to sea out of the cradle you! I was eleven.

I had a little suit of yellow oil clothes my father bought me. I went upstairs with him in Knickle's shop to see what I was goin' to get, you know. An' they was right yellow too an' they looked some nice. I thought, "Now here's somethin'. I got somethin' here." I hauled 'em on to see how they looked, you know. Seventy-five cents a suit. Right golden yellow. When I saw that first suit I was all overjoyed. I thought I was some man then.

I crawled up in the top bunk to see how it was up there. I figured that that was quite a somethin' to get up an' lay in the top bunk. Thought I was a hell of a big feller in the top bunk.

The skipper come down to the wharf. "Why," he said, "you ain't goin' with?"

I said, "Yes I'm goin'."

"You look kind o' small," he said. I thought I was big – I was big enough, but young, you know. He said, "Do you think you can tie up a tops'l?"

I said, "Well, we'll find out when we get out."

Oh, my God. How foolish it all was . . . I found out before the trip was o'er that I had no slouch of a job. T'roater was the hardest job aboard of the vessel. You had to fork the fish across the deck, fork 'em back o'er the break, an' fork 'em in the ked an' t'roat 'em. Well, the header an' the splitter only had one job but you got two or three. It's impossible. You can't do it.

In them days you didn't grow up. We was rushed up. Rushed up, you.

When I first went to sea I knowed nothin'. Went as catchy – eleven years old. You had to learn from what you seen and what they showed you. If they showed you somethin' you had to get it. You'd get it pretty quick. Why the odd feller'd be good to you, sometimes you'd strike an odd feller that'd be a little good to you.

Old Charlie Johnson told me to make a mat for on the anchor – a braided mat you'd lay on the anchor to keep the jib sheets from chafin' on that. What they call a punch mat – that's the name of it. He used to keep a splittin' knife for a sheath knife . . . old Charlie. An' he come an' told me to make a mat. I said, "Now what do I know about makin' a mat?"

"Why, a punch mat," he said.

"Man," I said, "I don't know what you mean."

"You can't make a punch mat?"

I said, "Where would I learn to make a punch mat? This is my first trip to sea. If you know how to make one why don't you show me? An' maybe I can learn."

An' he showed me. "Now," he said, "I'm only goin' to show you once." Then he got some rope for me an' he made his'n. An' he said, "Now I'll make mine. An' you make yours same as I make mine." An' he had that sheath knife an' every time I'd make a mistake I got a strike o'er the hands with the sheath knife handle. An' don't think it didn't hurt. He hit hard . . . it hit hard enough that it hurt hard so's I'd catch on.

I wasn't long in catchin' on how to make a punch mat, I'll tell you that . . . I can make 'em yet.

The family of us was three boys an' three girls. And money wasn't very plenty at that . . . them times. An' it wasn't no choices to make. You had to go . . . to try to keep the rest alive, you might say. I remember plenty times, an' I'm not tellin you no lie, that we left home to go fishin' that all the money was left in the house was thirty dollars, an' that had to do till that trip was up . . . three months.

And, by God, you worked for what you got. You get out an' you get way down below the vessel . . . if you get down with seven or eight tubs o' trawl an' start to pull back in a sou'easter in double handed dory . . . you don't know what it's like till you get there. You stand there an' you pull an' she strikes into the lop . . . an' you pull an' you pull an you don't make no headway. But you got to keep at it till you get aboard.

Why look! I often think, when I was thirteen years old, I was in the bow of a dory doin' a man's work. Now you got fellers walkin' around here nineteen, twenty years old, that never done a stroke o' work in their life . . . an' never intend to.

I was pretty young . . . thirteen years old. An' goin' to school I didn't like very much. I hated to go to school. So . . . my father, he used to go away Bank fishin'. And . . . well, the idea was, if I didn't like to go to school, why, I had to . . . I had to do somethin' else. So he said, "If you ain't satisfied to go to school, why you'll have to go 'way – go 'way fishin' . . . 'board the schooner."

Well this talk was goin' on t'rough the winter when everybody was home – my father he wasn't fishin' the winter season. Anyways, I didn't pay much attention to it – I thought he was jokin'. So when it come on towards spring, why as far as I could see, my mother, she was pickin' up some different kinds o' clothes for me, gettin' things ready, an' . . . an' after a while I come to see what was goin' to happen. Well . . . then I didn't feel so good, you.

So, in them years in the spring, why, you always started then for to go away to The Banks – the schooners that were ready used to go away on what they call the frozen baitin'. So . . . we went away . . . I went as what they call header, that was workin' on deck takin' the heads off the fish. An' Dad was in a dory wit' another feller – trawlin'. The next summer, my father, he decided for to go what they call handlinin' – one man to a dory. You went in a single dory – trawlin' was two men in a dory, handlinin' was one man. So that's how I got started off in the dories . . . quite an undertakin' at my age for to start off in a dory alone like that y'know. An' I got along pretty good . . . I had pretty good nerve, you, an' caught a good share o' fish. So, that summer handlinin' – an' then next summer, my dad he took me trawlin'. I went in the dory wit' him . . . an' that's the way I kept on. It wasn't . . . wasn't like goin' to school, you.

It was lots o' times that you didn't feel so good I'll tell you, was lots o' times that you got caught in a bad spot and you knowed you had some pretty narrow escapes, but you really didn't know at all how . . . how handy you was sometimes. You didn't really know.

My father an' I one time had a pretty narrow escape. It was the same year that he took me in the dory wit' him, trawlin'. That same season. I was only young. We come home off the summer trip an' the skipper, he decided to go down on what they call a fall trip, trawlin'. And, we went. It was out o' Riverport there wit' Lemmy Ritcey. An' he was a hard man too – I was wit' him five years. He wasn't only that high, but I'll tell you he had some spunk. He was a hard man for a little feller. Never looked 'round for anyt'ing, you.

Well, we went down there on a fall trip an' we was out there fishin' a while. So this one mornin' we turned out an' got our breakfasts an' we seen it was blowin' a good breeze. An' nobody didn't feel like goin'. Dories was still on deck y'know an' . . . an' everybody knowed it wasn't fit to go. So, the skipper, he seen that nobody was goin' to make any move to go you see, to get the dories off. An' after a while he started to come ahead from back aft, from the cabin. Got out the dory tackle. You know what that was – that was shovin' you along. So then, everybody started to take a'hold an' . . . we started to get the dories off the deck. An' we left for to haul our trawls – they was right around the vessel y'know, set right around the vessel. An' my father an' I, our trawl was set down to the leeward – right down to the stern o' the vessel.

Well, we had to go down – we had to go off to our outside buoy an' haul towards the vessel. So we run down – it was so much wind then we couldn't carry our sail – we run right off for our buoy. An' we got down, an' we got a'hold of our buoy . . . it kept all the time gettin worse, gettin' worse. Well, we . . . we got I guess pretty well half of it hauled. An' snap!– we parted our trawl. It was blowin' so hard the trawl parted. There we was . . . adrift . . . an' blowin' a livin' gale. Couldn't make no headway towards the vessel – all we could do was take our paddles an' try to keep the dory, y'know, hold her head to it. After a while it got so damn bad that my father had to go to work an' make what they call a droge to put out ahead for to try to help to hold her up an' break the seas. Took some trawl tubs an' sail, tied 'em onto the painter an' threw that out o'er the bow so when the dory pulled onto it y'see it kind of helped her into the wind – kept her from gettin' crossways into the seas. So . . . that's the way we kept on. The vessel lay to anchor an' all the time we was driftin' away from her. An' we wasn't parted off too long before we couldn't see the vessel no more. Dad, he didn't say anyt'in' at the time. An' I was only young – I didn't know too much. I didn't fear too much or think too much I guess. But Dad . . . well, he often talked about it afterwards. He said he figured that our end was comin' 'cause . . . well, he experienced so much in his life that . . . he thought he seen the end comin' . . . for the two of us.

Anyways it was blowin' so hard that Dad had to – had some line there in the dory – had to go to work an' cut off a piece o' line an' fasten it across our t'olpins, you know, for to keep the oars in place, so they wouldn't blow away. An' the seas! One time it was a sea struck the dory an' almost took Dad right out o'er the stern. He was in the stern o' the dory an' I was in the bow. Seas breakin' in o'er the dory . . . you had to keep your eyes around to keep from gettin' washed o'erboard. All you could do was just try to keep the dory straight . . . let 'er go . . . an' bail to keep the seas comin' in from swampin' her. I never been in a worse spot . . . an' I fished for a good many years.

Anyways, the other dories, they all got aboard. By luck they got aboard. So sure enough after a long, long time t'rough a good man . . . he had good nerve and good spirit, as you say it . . . . The skipper never mentioned a word about cuttin' the cable off . . . for to let the vessel come down to look for us. He never said a word. But they took over. This man an' another feller – an' the one man told the other feller – he said, "You go back in the cabin," he said, "an' get the axe." And, he took over . . . the skipper never said a word. Well, that was quite a somethin' . . . they cut the cable off, chopped 'er off. Chopped 'er right off. An' there was so much wind then they never put no sail on. They swung 'er off stern to it. An' a feller – Joey Wentzel from o'er there in Riverport – he was up to the crosstrees, he shinned up there for to look.

Joey t'ought that he sighted us – he sighted somethin', but he wasn't sure. They was goin' to give it up, mind you. They was goin' to give it up. The skipper said, "It's no use to go any further."

Well, Joey said, "I'm not sure, I think, I believe I see somethin'." They kept comin'. An' by an' by Joey was sure that he seen us. An' they kept comin'. An' by God, she come that we could see her. Well, we had pretty good nerve then. They was runnin' off the wind. No sail or not'in' on. An' she was comin'.

An' then they got down to us. They got down to the leeward of us an' they untied the fores'l, took the stops off – brand new fores'l – we bent on a brand new fores'l right out o' the sail loft that fall before we left home. An' they went to hoist it, see, so the schooner would lay for us to get aboard . . . an' it just made one slap an' the whole t'ing went right out of the ropes. One slap, you . . . that new canvas tore right out of the ropes. Not'in' left. Brand new sail. Now you know what it was like. So, they had to leave 'er lay then . . . had to leave 'er lay, driftin' 'er off sideways. And we . . . we managed to get along side. An' they reached down an' grabbed us. They reached down an' I can feel it yet . . . got me by the back o' the neck. We was all in, you understand. We wasn't fit for anyt'ing. My two hands . . . they was all . . . every finger an' across the palms here was big blisters. From pullin' you y'know, holdin' onto the oars . . . all big blood blisters. A state, an awful state, you. Awful mess we was into. By luck we got saved, we got aboard . . . all right. I don't know how it happened, but . . . we got saved. That was a hard drill. Yes, that was a hard drill. Dad, he often talked about it afterwards. In my whole time o' goin' I haven't seen much worse an' I was only young then.

One year here . . . I don't know how many people got lost . . . oh, my . . . in 1926. Six vessels, I believe. My son was very near aboard one of the boats.

The first time they come down I kind o' promised he would go. We was on the field ploughin'.

They come down for to get him on the second day. But as luck happened . . . he was gone up to town to get some seed for the spring plantin'. Somethin' held him up. Whatever it was I don't know. They wouldn't wait any longer, see. In a rush, you know – they said the skipper wanted to get off today.

They went down an' got Johnny Wagner's two boys. Both went as t'roaters. Two boys in the place of one – twelve and fifteen years old. No experience on vessels.

The two of them got lost. That was a heavy storm . . . oh my . . . the vessel . . . all hands gone.

28923

# No Slackin' Back

Now you take forty odd vessels from the river here – twenty men on a vessel – that was some men from around here. Most o' the men off the islands here used to go . . . they'd all have their dories home, you see. That was handy. I'd take my dory home – the vessel dory, belonged to the vessel. An' then I'd have her all fitted up – a sail made an' everythin' – all rigged up for fishin'. An' the vessels, they used to come down the river an' lay off o' Mosher's Head . . . for to pick up the men from the islands. Used to see her flag . . . we were watchin' . . . an' when we seen her comin' then we'd row down an' go aboard of her. Hoist the dories aboard an' nest 'em . . . an' go off to The Banks. Bring our bed clothes down, you – all straw sacks them times we used, sacks filled with straw – put 'em aboard the vessel. An' chests – we used to use all chests for clothes an' gear an' so on. I can see the dories yet, comin' through the channel . . . a lot of 'em. An' that was how we left for The Banks.

Handlinin', when you leave home you'd have eighteen dories. Well that'd be eighteen men fishin' in dories. One man in a dory . . . two if you was trawlin'. Well then you have a dress gang . . . that'd be header, an' t'roater, an' splitter would be three, cook'd be four. Cap'n be five. That'd be twenty-three in crew all together. Well you'd take food supplies an' water – enough to last you to catch a trip o' fish. Somewheres between two, three months. Well then we'd go fish around Querro, Western Bank, an' Sable Island. When you was fishin' handlinin', you was fishin' on count. The more fish you caught, the more money you made. You caught the fish with a handline, an' each feller counted his fish . . . each feller competin' with the next. Trawlin' was settled up on shares but handlinin' you was out on count an' that made it all the worse. They wouldn't stop to eat or nothin', y'know, some of 'em.

They come aboard to get their dinner an' they had soup . . . well they just drunk it right out o' the plates. They was full o' rushin' – one feller tryin' to beat the other. It was every feller for himself. If you didn't know nothin', don't ask. Don't ask me because I won't tell you. You had to learn all that yourself. If I tell you somethin' about fishin', well then maybe you'll get more of a count than me. That was the nick. The owners had it figured that way – to get more fish . . . put one man against the other, see. It was one of the crookedest ways of fishin' that any man could do. If you didn't catch very many fish, you didn't make much money . . . an' there was a high line an' a low line in that racket.

The last year I was with Wallace Conrad in the *Bernard B. Conrad* we had twenty-one hundred quintals o' fish. An' that's a lot o' fish. A hundred an' twelve pounds to the quintal – that's dried. Salted an' dried. An' that's how the haul was given. Washed 'em an' dried 'em on the flakes when we got home. Anyways, there was one man had more fish n' what I had – sixty-eight fish more than what I had. An' his name was Albert Conrad – lives in LaHave. So it was about a few days before Christmas, we settled. I made a hundred an' eighty-three dollars. Albert – he was high line – he made a hundred an' eighty-five. Made two dollars more than what I did. Low line made ninety-six. That's for three months work, you. Three months of hard work . . . damn hard work . . . your sore hands . . . the blood runnin' out of 'em sometimes from haulin'. Broke open here in the joints an' blood runnin' right out of 'em. I seen us when it took seven of us to hoist one end of a dory onto the vessel . . . when one feller could do it when his hands ain't sore. But you had to keep at it as far as that goes . . . you was out there for a livin' and you had to keep at it.

Now when you're trawlin' one man stands in the bow o' the dory and he's haulin' the trawl in . . . trawl hauls over a little roller. An' when a gangin' comes up wit' a fish onto it why he just gives it a slap to get the hook free. An' then the other feller – feller in the stern – he's got a tub there settin' between his legs full o' bait, an' he baits the hook an' passes it out o'er the other side. That's what you call an underrun. An' that's the way that goes till you shift to another ground . . . then the buoys an' the trawl anchors got to come in an' the trawl lines got to be coiled an' taken aboard the vessel.

An' when you was out in them dories you wanted a lot o' judgement I'll tell you that . . . plenty o' judgement to find your marker buoy . . . an' to keep from goin' astray from the vessel altogether. Now, the vessel, she'd be swingin' around her anchor wit' the tides . . . an' your inside buoy'd be off some . . . oh maybe as much as a quarter of a mile to keep your trawl free of the vessel. Then wit' four tubs o' trawl set it'd be another mile an' sometimes more to your outside buoy. Most generally you'd haul from that outside buoy an' come up towards the vessel. Sail down to your outside buoy . . . haul against the wind, see. An' then row back wit' your load o' fish. Of course, the ones that's up ahead o' the vessel, to the wind'ard o' the vessel, they'd start haulin' an' go away from the vessel. They'd sail back then . . . they'd have a free tow back. Now the outside buoy'd have a staff onto it an' a flag . . . an' there was plenty o' times a feller'd miss that buoy in the fog or if it was blowin' . . . or snow t'ick. See when you set out you'd take your course from the vessel – dories all carried a compass – take your course an' while you was rowin' you count your strokes . . . you want to make sure you count your strokes. Every time you pull back, that's one. An' if you was sailin' you're settin' on the t'wart countin' just the same as when you're rowin' – "One . . . two . . . " an' you count that way till you t'ink you're down to the buoy . . . so many hundred strokes. Do that on each run see, on each haul . . . you'd make three or four hauls a day. Haul up four times a day, most generally.

An' if it's blowin' hard, you got to allow yourself so much leeway one way or the other. An' say there's a tide runnin' to the west'ard an' you're goin' for your buoy east or sou'east – the tide's runnin' to the west'ard, you got to allow so much for your tide. A couple points on your compass for tide – tide takin' you this way, you got to steer that way. An' when you miss the buoy . . . if you didn't see it, you'd start zigzaggin' back an' forth. A hundred strokes one way an' a hundred strokes anot'er way, hundred strokes back an' that's the way you'd zigzag – like a saw tooth. So far each way . . . all the time countin' your strokes, see. An' sometimes you'd miss it altogether . . . if you didn't see it, you'd have to row back to the vessel . . . try again.

I can say we had some good times aboard the vessels . . . but I'll tell you, the bad times made up for the good ones. Sometimes the weather'd be black t'ick o' fog an' you had a whole string o' trawl out. You'd go in your dory then before breakfast – make a run for your marker buoy an' you'd miss it. An' you'd have to turn around an' row back to the vessel for to take your course again. Sometimes you'd be at your first haul . . . start out before the sun was up . . . be at your first haul for four hours . . . wit' nothin' to eat. I remember one day, my dory mate an' me missed our buoy six times. Whatever was wrong, I don't know. You're behind all day . . . an' it makes awful hard work. There was never no slackin' back. Never.

Well, I'll tell you how it went for me one year . . . the year I made my fortune! I was wit' Hector Sperry up here – my wife's brother there – him an' I went in a dory together. We got along fine. We was gone a month or more on the frozen baitin'. When we got home here . . . them times you had to make all your fish, dry 'em you understand. Was no sellin' 'em right fresh. An' we landed down here on what they call Mullock's Beach. We got in here early in the mornin' an' we started right in takin' out fish. Some o' the men would boat fish ashore, an' others'd be ashore, you know, pilin' 'em up an' layin' 'em out onto the flakes. I was ashore pilin' fish an' the skipper was comin' around seein' who'd be on the next trip wit' him. He come up to me, he said, "You're goin' wit' me next trip?"

"I'll go back wit' you, old man," I said, "I'll stay for the season." An' he was all tickled. So anyway, I done so. I was kind o' happy about it . . . only young an' just startin' out, see.

An' we went down onto what they call the spring trip . . . we was gone around two months on that trip. Fished herring – fresh bait for trawlin' on the spring trip. Picked up the herrin' in Queensport, you see, an' went off to The Banks for to set trawl. So we come home – well then we got our money for our frozen baitin'. That's the way they done it see – settled up for the first trip after we come home from the next trip. We made forty dollars.

So we was home here about a week or so, I guess until the vessel was fitted out to go down on the summer trip. Started out for Newfoundland for capelin – capelin was our bait, you understand. We went out to The Banks on our summer trip an' we never done anyt'in' a'tall. None o' the vessels didn't do hardly anyt'in' that summer. An' after capelin gets o'er . . . well then the squid come. You got to fish squid when the capelin gets o'er. An' squid was scarce that summer too . . . no bait an' no fish. We had no fish . . . an' we was down there almost t'ree months. So when we got home here . . . well, we settled up for our spring trip. Made seventy-t'ree dollars on the spring trip. Awful big money!

An' to top it all off, sometime t'rough the winter – I don't know just when it was, sometime just after Christmas . . . one day I went to the post office. An' there was a letter for me. I never opened it until I got home . . . an' when I got home I opened it up. I looked at the check . . . settlement for the summer trip, you understand. I thought it was twenty-nine dollars. I took a second look at it . . . it was twenty-nine cents! That's true as I sit here. Twenty-nine cents. That was after my expenses . . . I had my tobacco bill to pay for an' a suit of oil clothes. I had twenty-nine cents. Now there was a summer's work wasn't it!

Made a little o'er a hundred dollars for the whole season. Well . . . it was all right for me – I was only young. That was my first year in the dory. But there was an awful lot o' men aboard that was married an' had big families. All winter . . . well I tell you it was damn hard . . . for the men that had families. I was only young then an' took what I made. You take it . . . nothin' much you could do. Ones that had families, they was really up against it that winter.

We fished in all kinds o' weather, you. Made no difference. I was out in the dory different times when you couldn't see your fish till it come t'rough the ice. That's slop ice – ice just startin' to form. Ca'm water an' no wind – the ice just startin' to form on the water like slush. That's salt water freezin', mind you. Some say it ain't suppose to freeze but I know different. An' the fish when you hauled him up, his nose come t'rough the ice. Cold . . . cold . . . I don't know how we ever done it. Some fellers hauled the trawl bare handed. Some fellers fainted too, you know.

The skipper'd send you out as long as you could get out – long as you could get the dories off an' get out. Some of 'em was pretty rusty characters . . . hardly ever stop you from goin' off. He'd care only about the fish . . . and he's sleepin' while you was out haulin'. The one Cap'n I was with – he kept a dog aboard, see. There was many a night . . . blowin' a gale an' stormin' . . . why he'd call that dog in an' leave the men out. The men were out an' they'd stay out . . . on deck or in the dories. Made no difference to him. He must o' lost seven or eight men when I was with him . . . more or less.

This once he dropped us off to haul our gear on what you call a flyin' set . . . he drops one dory off, then goes so far an' he drops anot'er one an' so on. Then you take your course for your trawl an' he's got to sail down on the wind'ard end to follow you along an' take the dories aboard after you got your gear into the dory. See, the dories are all set out in a string an' the vessel has to come back for to pick you up. Anyways, he must have been three parts drunk. All the other vessels that were around us never had a dory off of the deck a'tall . . . the wind nor'west when we set out. An' it was dirty – snowin' an' blowin'. We had quite a few fish an' we had all our gear . . . we was loaded down an' the gunnels wasn't far out of the water. An' that son of a bitch come down along an' almost run us down. God Almighty knows how many men that man lost.

Now, when I was fishin', some fellers used to say about this one skipper – about how hard he was . . . used his men bad, see. Well, I heard about this Cap'n an' I said to myself, I said, "You can't kill me. I'm goin' to try you out." Got down there on The Grand Banks – the weather was just breakin' up – was the last o' March, gettin' fine. An' we set out ten dories on a flyin' set. An' the last dory what he dropped off was on the fish, was on the halibut, see. But the first dory – an' she was a ways off – there was no halibut there. An' he wouldn't go back to pick that dory up. He made them men pull the whole length of them ten dories. They never got aboard till into the evenin'. Half o' the dories . . . five dories got aboard you see, an' we baited the trawl an' set out the other way – where the halibut was. An' he made them men pull the whole distance. Well that'd be a long ways wit' the tide – would be t'ree miles or more.

An' one time he said we'd make a set up here handy to home, see. Come up on middle ground. An' we set the trawl that afternoon. An' we couldn't haul back . . . breezed up nor'east, was snowin'. Now sometime t'rough the night he said we'd get it . . . haul back. Well, we said – you know, all the men got down together talkin' – we said, "What are we goin' to do? Go out? Go out in the night to haul trawl in a snowstorm?"

"Oh," he says, "it's moonlight out."

An' at two o'clock the wind died down a little. But it was still snowin'. He said, "We'll go out. Blow the horn to get out." We got out. An' it was rough too. I'm tellin' you, it was rough – spittin' an' snowin'. An' I told my dory mate, "Look," I said, "I'm not goin' to look for no halibut." I said, "Whatever comes in, comes in, an' what goes out will stay out." An' we got the trawl – we got it pretty fast too. The vessel, she used to jog away from us, you know. But we had a torch. An' we had that on the trawl tub y'know so's we could get a readin' off the compass – follow the vessel wit' the compass, you understand. We watched the vessel goin', how she was joggin'. An' we got the trawl an' we got over to her, an' got aboard. Two o'clock in the night . . . in a snowstorm. We never lost a man though.

After a while the owner o' the vessel wouldn't give her to him no more – wouldn't give him the vessel. He'd drown all the men. That's right! Drown 'em all – crazy, that's all he was. Only reason men went wit' him was he used to get so many fish. High liner see. But the man was crazy. In his time sailin' as master he lost, I know, upwards of eighteen men – fishin' in all kinds of weather. He was crazy, you. Right crazy.

Dory fishin' was disgustin' – a disgustin' job. A fearful disgustin' job. To go down there in that hold with the frost hangin' down – icicles hangin' down o'erhead from the deck planks. Go down there to bait up five tubs of gear to a dory. And you stayed down there till you had it baited up – till the cook blowed the whistle for breakfast about half past two or three o'clock in the mornin'. Gettin' to the table was a race, like a race, you know, all a race – one feller tryin' to get ahead of the other. You'd go down an' get your breakfast an' soak it into you – hot biscuits, an' fried potatoes, an' pork sausages, eggs – plenty of it . . . eat all you want. Around breakfast you'd be about done baitin' up then. The second table gang'd be pretty near finished baitin' up while the first table gang was eatin'. Then you'd go back down an' finish baitin' trawl.

You'd be settin' down in the fo'c's'le – when the wind's blowin' a good breeze – an' maybe you couldn't get right off – waitin' with your gear all baited up, not daylight yet, dark an' waitin'. Layin' around wet and your oil clothes on. And waitin' for a feller to come along an' sing out, "Get up your tubs, boys!" Couldn't take your oil clothes off on account of might set the next minute – the next minute, the next half-hour – waitin' for that. When the wind's blowin' a good strong breeze – waitin' . . . find out what you was goin' to do before you laid in the bunk. An' sometimes no set at all. Layin' around all day wet an' your oil clothes on. No system of any kind. No regulation, no system whatever. No.

Then when the call did come you'd hoist the dories out an' hang 'em out o'er the side. An' if you was on the wind'ard side . . . more than once I shut my eyes. The fellers on the deck would let the dory fly. If the vessel made a roll to the leeward you was up about twenty feet. An' if you fetched up against the vessel . . . if your tongue was between your teeth, you'd bite your tongue off! An' the feller in the bow had a piece o' rope fastened to the riggin' o' the vessel an' drove t'rough the strap o' the dory. An' he held straight onto that, you see, until they got her clear. The feller that let the dory go, he grabbed the hook an' unhooked 'em . . . till the eight or ten dories was out. An' many's the mornin' you'd drop off three, four o'clock in the mornin' wit' the vessel goin' along about four, five miles an hour – that's how we set. A flyin' set, they called it. Would drop one on one side an' one on the other. In the dark an' you couldn't see nothin'.

Then you had a course to row. If the wind was blowin' west, you'd set out an' go maybe sou'east. That's right off the wind. In the dark! Well, you'd make your run down an' if you find your buoy, fine. But if you didn't find your buoy . . . go back to the vessel an' go again. An' sometimes if it was fog t'ick or blowin' you'd make maybe two, three trips before you'd find your trawl buoy . . . a mile down an' a mile back. Four hauls a day . . . in the dory four times a day wit' several miles o' gear ahead o' you. Sometimes it wasn't so good, you.

An' after you made your last haul of the day an' all them fish was forked up on deck, why then you'd go to work an' help the dress gang get the fish split an' salted down. An' if you was gettin' any amount o' fish, why you had some pile o' work ahead o' you . . . you dasn't waste any time. The most time that I had to spend out was . . . at one time . . . was seventy-two hours wit'out a wink . . . we was on our feet goin' right straight, goin' right straight – seventy-two hours. Lots o' fish, see. Never saw the bunk, you. An' that last set we made . . . it was a short set in the mornin', an' we got the gear back . . . don't think we wasn't tickled! Got straightened away, got cleaned up an' got straightened away . . . that was a hard, hard, hard trip. 'Course most trips wasn't that hard, but I can say that you never got no over amount o' sleep on them vessels. You might get a good run of fish for five, six days or somethin' . . . and boys, you wouldn't see much of your bunk. Why if a man set down, he wasn't no more n' set down – asleep. Fall asleep . . . so played out, y'know, tired, cold, an' one t'ing an' anot'er. I seen lots o' times that . . . a feller'd be forkin' fish an' over tired – the minute he'd stop he'd go right head first. Into the fish he was forkin', you! Why, I seen a man wit' a splittin' knife that he'd split a fish an' before he'd get a chance to reach for anot'er one he'd . . . he'd make a nod an' be dead to the world. Dead to the world, you.

Then, of course, after all them fish was dressed down, why if you was lucky you had an hour's watch yet that night! Why, you'd have to stand that – take turns, you understand – your hour's watch. An' next mornin' be at the whole t'ing again. An' that's how it went . . . you had to go . . . if the rest went. If you hung back sayin', "I'm not goin'," – the first rock they'd get to, they'd chase you ashore. You just had to work hard as you could an' go along an' try to get a dollar. It was never endin', you. I remember . . . there was times when two or t'ree hours rest . . . would of meant everyt'ing.

One time I was with Cap'n Wilbert Fralich in the *Ocean Maid* up in the North Bay, an' I was cook. We had a young feller from Mount Pleasant back here. And he didn't like the sea, he didn't like the water. He wanted to get home. "Cook," he said, "what must I do to get home?"

Well I said, "You can't do anythin'." I said, "You're here. And you got to stay here till the trip's up."

He said, "I'm goin' to cut my finger off."

"You're crazy," I said.

And at that time, you know, we had wood for to make fire into the ship's stove. He went down an' we had a hatchet for splittin'. I was rollin' out some cookies or doin' somethin'. First thing I heard maybe a coupl'a hacks with the axe. He come up an' said, "Cook, I cut my finger off." He cut it off back'a that joint there, the far finger.

I run up for the Cap'n an' he come down to see the boy. An' the Cap'n, back he went you – fainted! Well I rolled 'im around a coupl'a times an' he come to, his head hangin' down. I said, "The boy cut his finger off. What are you goin' to do about it?"

"Fix him up, cook, as best you can."

Well, I fetched him back an' tied a rag onto his finger. Poured a bottle of iodine right in the cut. He kicked for a while. I'm goin' to tell you, he kicked!

And we had to take him to land. Put him ashore in Souris. We landed him, he went home. And he got home. He got clear.

He hated it that much. He didn't want to be on the water.

Why it was inhuman. Set out in t'ick o' fog – snow t'ick which it often was. Out an' set the trawl in blizzards – it would snow – snow your torch out. You had a torch lit you know – a piece of pipe wit' a wick shoved down, filled wit' kerosene. An' there was a clasp on the side of it – you hooked that on the trawl tub. An' that was flickerin' in your eyes, blindin' you that you couldn't see nothin', nothin' but the torch. An' when the torch'd go out you had to set in the dark – you'd have to set in the dark an' that meant a lot o' snarls when you hauled back. Well, when you got your trawl set you'd come aboard an' got what they call a mug-up – a lunch – then you'd go out an' haul back an' come back an' get your dinner an' maybe you'd be back at twelve o'clock for your dinner but probably it'd be five or six in the evenin'. You didn't know what was what. But you was goin' to do what you could do. There was nothin' good that you could look into any of it. No you couldn't see nothin' that looked anyways bright a'tall.

You get your trawl – it was loaded wit' fish, why then you knowed you had a damn lot o' hard work. It looked bright – you had the fish all right – it was labour to get 'em off. I seen it quite often when there was practically one on every hook an' there was about five-thousand hooks on that trawl an' you knowed what fish was on. I helped to bring ten dory loads in down on The Grand Banks in one day – ten loads! Come to the vessel ten times. 'Course that don't happen very often. When you get a lot o' fish in your trawl like that, that makes hard work because your trawl hauls hard – that many fish got to make your trawl haul hard. The only thing that's bright in it is you know you're gettin' some fish. But you know you're not goin' to get no money. You'd get no money 'cause there was none to get. A cent, cent an' a half a pound. When they started to pay you a cent an' a half a pound for haddock, I said, "Boys, we got to sharpen our gaffs up. We dasn't let none go – got to hook 'em all!" A cent an' a half, you.

Used to figure about quittin' all the time. But listen you, somethin'd give you a little courage for the next trip. That's the only t'ing that helped it out. I was at it forty-odd years.

Out on The Banks there I remember . . . we got through dressin' fish at half past one o'clock in the mornin'. Been fishin' steady for forty-three hours. Lots o' fish runnin', see. Baitin' trawl, settin' trawl an' haulin' trawl – forty-three hours, you. Never had a wink o' sleep. An' some o' the men, they fell right asleep where they was . . . at what they was workin' at . . . dressin' fish. I run down aft – thought the Cap'n'd give us two hours sleep . . . you know, before we baited up the trawl again. I said, "We loaded all the fish down, old man." He looked at me. He was asleep in the chair. He woke up there a little bit. Looked at me kind o' sleepy, you.

"This gang wouldn't stand it on Saint Pierre Bank – the way we fished there years ago."

I said, "What do you mean?"

"Well," he said, "you wouldn't stand it – we fished night an' day."

"The only difference I can see," I said, "between here an' Saint Pierre Bank is the tide makes the trawl haul a lot harder here than it did at Saint Pierre's. That's all the difference."

"Bait 'em up," he said, "bait 'em up." Had no mercy on anybody, you. There was no turnin' out or turnin' in. You was out.

An' when Sunday come, that was it. There was no fishin' done on Sunday on board of them vessels. Oh, we might go out on deck an' study the tide – see how the tide run around with the sun. An' what time it changed. But no fishin' – an' the Cap'n, if he seen you put a line down for bait – squid – boys, he'd go after you. You'd get quite a callin' down. We never fished on Sundays.

We'd have a shave up, you see, clean up – you wouldn't shave all week. Clean up on Sundays. After you cleaned up an' ate breakfast you might take a nap. An' when Sunday afternoon come, well, you used to get together an', there was fellers that would sing an' some of 'em used to have accordions an' violins an' we'd have a sing-song. If you could sing, you would help to sing an' some feller'd play the violin, you see. Them old fellers wit' the violin could play good. I know one year there wit' Cap'n Dan Romkey, we had two Newfoundland men. An' the one, well his name was Sam White an' boys he could certainly play the accordion. An' then there was anot'er man – he had his violin wit'. An' they used to play the accordion an' violin together an' they used – a lot o' the men used to sing, the fellers what could sing good. An' them old hymns. They used to sing to pass the evenin' away . . . it was very nice. An' the fellers what couldn't sing, why they enjoyed it maybe more so than the fellers that was singin'. We all hands sat around, you, an' we certainly enjoyed it. See, there was no radios or nothin' for to listen at . . . an' you made your own entertainment.

So we'd have singin' an' we'd say grace . . . well some religious fellers we'd have aboard would say grace at the table – you know, the blessin'. An' the cook, he used to soak out salt meat. An' he used to roast it. Soak it out fresh, an' then he'd roast it for Sunday dinner. Roast it for Sunday an' he'd make a big cake an' put a lot o' frostin' on it – it was some good.

But today it ain't like that. It's just an endless chain – goes right around. These fellers on the draggers here think they're doin' good fishin' on Sunday, but they're not. They're losin'. They're losin' on the other end.

# Ain't on Much Land

I suppose we were scared more than once on the vessels. When you go away you don't think about . . . that you ain't goin' to get home again. You don't think about that. When you got into a heavy storm . . . well then maybe you'd think onto it. But after the storm was o'er, it'd all go away from you. An' when you went in the next year, when the next year'd come . . . you were just as anxious to go back as you ever was before.

You'd forget about the hard times. You had to forget about 'em. 'Cause if you didn't, well you'd be no good . . . if you kept thinkin' about it an' thinkin' about it. . . . Wasn't much use to be afraid . . . I guess sometimes . . . well, the best in you would put the good side out. The harder it blowed the more courage you got . . . I always had good courage when it blowed.

If you got afraid an' I got afraid an' somebody else got afraid, you understand . . . well, first thing it was t'ree parts of us afraid. Nobody would go on deck to do anyt'ing then. You'd be down below an' the vessel'd be goin' 'round in circles! What was the biggest vessels? A hundred an' forty? You're on a hundred an' forty feet an' you ain't on much land. An' out joggin' around in a dory day in an' day out . . . you get scared sometimes, don't worry. But you don't let it out . . . like I told you . . . one dasn't tell the other because you'd all give up. No sir, we didn't t'ink of no danger. Jumped in the dory an' let 'er go. Wit' a watch in your pocket an' a compass – an' let 'er go. That's the only t'ing you could do . . . if you was to make a good job of it.

'Course there was many a time a vessel'd come in home here wit' the flag at half-mast . . . see, if they lost a man or two men – whatever it was – they'd have the flag just halfways down from the top o' the topmast to the crosstrees. Halfways to the cross. See on them big vessels we used to have a mainmast 'round eighty-five to ninety foot. Then there was a topmast, top o' that – oh, thirty-five or forty feet, I guess. Crosstrees at where the topmast joined onto the mainmast. An' when they lost a man, they come in wit' the flag flyin' there halfways above the cross.

I remember one time I was wit' Loren Ritcey. I sailed a lot wit' Loren – him an' I. I broke him in a dory – took him in a dory first. An' then he got far enough advanced that he got his own vessel – skipper.

But this day we were . . . oh, I would say it was way into the middle o' February. We made a set an' the wind hauled here sou'east. I don't know how much trawl we set but it wasn't a whole lot . . . wind was sou'east an' that's not a very good wind. Well we made one set an' we made for to come in home. We had the fish dressed an' was gettin' things straightened up for to go in. An' I was standin' aft by the pilot house. Loren Ritcey was up there steerin' an' I was standin' back there cleanin' out my compass bucket . . . cleanin' out my compass bucket. Savin' only for that, Pearly Lohnes wouldn't be here today.

I went to pour the water out o' my bucket an' I looked o'er the rail. Jesus! Here's a man goin' back by the side. An' I sung out the alarm, "One o' the men o'erboard! Let 'er come up." A sou'east wind an' the way he was comin' he was runnin' right off the wind y'know. An' Loren, he give 'er the wheel, brought 'er hard up, an' then he could see him. An' I run for'ard an' they . . . they was all standin' there one lookin' at the other. They got . . . they knew what they should do but they couldn't. They was just standin' there. An' I says, "Quick get the dory o'er! Cut the ropes! Get the gripes off!" So we got the gripes off, an' the cord, an' got the dory onto the rail an' out o'erboard. An' I don't know now if there was two or t'ree jumped in the dory. An' God, when they got pretty near to him, his dory mate made kind of a run. An' God they run o'er him! He was underneat' the bottom o' the dory. An' when he come t'rough under the dory, Clyde Conrad – that was his uncle – he reached down as far as he could reach an' he just could reach him. He had a sou'wester on an' that's one thing that saved him. Hooked him underneat' the bottom of his sou'wester an' pulled him up . . . they got him in the dory.

Well now, in the middle o' February, you know the water is not very warm. Especially now on deck an' cold before you hit the water. They put him aboard . . . got him down an' got dry clothes for him. An' they put him in the bunk. An' I think that was all the quilts that was in the fo'c's'le, they had o'er him. Somebody had some brandy – gave him a glass o' that. He was so chilled he was right numb. But he survived. Well, that's the way things goes from that . . . you come against some queer ups an' downs in fishin'.

Me an' Angus Heckman o'er here, we was in the dory together . . . in the *Bluenose* wit' Angus Walters. We was trawlin' down on The Grand Banks. It was a dirty evenin' . . . dirty lookin' evenin'. T'underin' an' lightnin' heavy. He sent us out to make a run – well, he didn't send us out. We went. But he didn't stop us. The second hand got to do with that. He thinks it ain't fit to go why he'd to to the master an say, "Why, I don't t'ink, old man, it's fit to go." You know, the second hand's got to look after that. And that's what puts the second hand in the wrong a lot o' times, you. Well, he didn't stop us from goin' out an' it was too bad to be out. He should'a knowed it. An' the skipper should'a knowed it.

It wasn't fit . . . wasn't fit to go. We went. We had some fresh squid. We'd like to get 'em on the gear – the trawl lines. And we went out.

Well we hauled up . . . we had a load o' fish, me and Angus . . . we had a load o' fish in the dory an' I said to Angus, "We got about fifteen, twenty pieces o' squid yet in the tub there." An' I said, "I t'ink we'll knock off, Angus, an' try to get up to the vessel." We was down a ways on the wind side of 'er. We had a nice little ways to buck . . . to pull, see.

Angus said, "We'll try to hook them few squid on that we got yet." He was baitin' an' I was haulin'. He said, "We'll hook them few baits on yet then we'll go."

I said, "I ain't takin' no more fish in the dory. Got fish enough."

And before he had them few squid hooked on, the sea broke. An' when it broke – I can see it yet – it combed right up, right hollow-like. An' the dory drove right down into it . . . wit' a load o' fish into it. Well, when she come out o' the sea . . . we hadn't a load o' fish, it was half of it washed into the sea. Lost o'erboard. Angus was back in the stern o' the dory . . . drove him back into the stern o' the dory. An' I was settin' on the for'ard t'wart. I told him, I said, "Grab for me the bait tub there." I said, "If you can, get that other bait tub out o' the trawl tub an' start bailin'." The dory was down – the gunnels was under water. The two gunnels . . . I looked . . . an' seen they was about two inches under water. It was no use to grab the fish an' t'row 'em o'er because that didn't go fast enough . . . it was too much water. The only chance I seen . . . the only chance was to bail. An' I told him to bail on the starboard side an' I bailed on the port side so we'd keep the dory a little level . . . so when she come out o' the water we'd have a chance.

And boys, I seen a dory pullin' up, off a little ways. Couldn't see no distance. I seen this dory a ways off an' I grabbed a paddle quick an' swung it up two or t'ree times – case he might see it, see . . . come o'er to us. He didn't see us. I throwed it down. We had no time for that.

I said to Angus, "Keep at it. Don't give up."

He said, "My God, we're gone."

And I said, "We're not gone. Keep bailin'. There's no use doin' anyt'ing else because they won't see us aboard the vessel. There's no use to holler because they won't hear us."

By an' by I seen the gunnels come out a little. I said, "Keep 'er goin' boys. We got to do it." And by God we got 'er clear. She was free you! I started to grab them big codfish – all them big steak cod – an' started to fire 'em o'erboard, o'er the sides. I didn't care if we had one fish in the dory then to go aboard. So we got 'er freed up an' bailed 'er out with the bailers.

We started to pull up. After a little bit we got up along side an' got aboard. Why the old man – the skipper, he come out an' he said, "What happened?"

"What happened! What happened! If you want to put dories out in a night like this you want to keep your eyes around, old man! You want to keep your eyes around in case somethin' does happen that you can do somethin' . . . or somebody can do somethin'," I said. "We almost drowned down here! We was all but sunk. We was there 'bout half an hour bailin' an' workin' for to get the dory free. An' you fellers up here aboard the vessel didn't look down an' see us . . . nobody to see us."

"Oh," he said, "that's the way them things happen."

"Yes, by God," I told him, "that's the way them things happen!"

"Go down and put on dry clothes," he said.

"No," I said, "the hell wit' dry clothes. I'll dress fish." I stayed up on deck. I was right on 'em till the fish was all done an' everyt'ing was under cover.

I'll tell you, a dory is really 'bout the best boat you can put on the water – they're on top of everythin'. 'Course when you get 'em loaded down wit' fish, say up to the risin's, there's not much freeboard out there – sometimes a couple, t'ree inches is all. That's what put the danger into it. When it's dirty, when it's blowin' hard, an' loppy – especially goin' off the wind, when you're runnin' off the wind – that's awfully tricky. See, when a lop strikes 'em, when you got fish in an' a big sea runnin' you're goin' to get some headway.

I only seen one man in my life that got lost in a dory. That was sou'east from the nor'west light on Sable Island. Sou'east – we were off there about ten miles, fishin'. An' I had a dorymate from Bridgewater – pretty hard egg, they told me how hard he was when I got aboard the vessel. An' I said, "The harder the man, the better I like 'im." Anyways, we had ten dories out. An' we went up on the wind'ard end. We was the last dory up – on a flyin' set. The tenth – was nine dories from ours down to the vessel.

An' well, the wind was sou'west, blowin' a pretty good breeze – an' the tide was goin' to the wind'ard. See, the tide goin' to the wind'ard – that made it so much choppier. We was gettin' a lot o' fish in the boat an' the wind wasn't slackin' off any. So my dory mate he says, "What do you t'ink of it?"

I said, "We got fish enough. We'd better cut," I said. "Cut the trawl an' put the buoy on. We got fish enough."

We seen it was gettin' loppier. Seen the vessel down there joggin' good – bowsprit pitchin' into the seas. Well, my dory mate he throwed me a keg an' he took the other keg. I knowed what that meant – if you fill the dory, take a'hold of the keg –

it'll help keep you afloat. We was in a hard spot – an' she was takin' some pretty high seas. Breezin' up all the time, you see.

I'll tell you that was some hard pull . . . . An' when we got down to the vessel, a little ways from 'er, we seen one feller up in the riggin', lookin', an' anot'er feller out on the bowsprit, lookin' at us fellers comin' down. They were afraid we were goin' to get lost too.

See, when we got aboard, they told us was a man gone. Two fellers in a dory – an' this sea come an' fetched 'er o'er. The one feller couldn't swim – an' the sea drug 'im away from the dory. An' the other feller . . . all he could do to hang on. Just an unlucky sea – an unlucky sea come along. An' see, this feller, he wasn't lookin', you know – he had his head down lookin' in the tub coilin' the trawl. If he'd'a been lookin', they could pay over the line an' get the bow more to it an' get clear. Just an unlucky sea . . . nobody's fault.

Well, when the fish was dressed down, we talked about it. A friend gone, see . . . we was feelin' some bad about it, you. We hadn't a very good feelin' on it. An'the Cap'n come down, Cap'n Walter Crouse – he was a good skipper, a gen'leman. He told us, "We're goin' in. We won't stay out. We'll come in an' report there's a man gone."

So that's what we done. It wasn't no good feelin' you know. Everybody felt pretty sad about it. You take right among a bunch o' men all the time an' then you lose a feller . . . it didn't feel very good. Well . . . you come in an' . . . it felt some bad to come in, you know, wit' your flag at half-mast. Heart breakin' t'ing that was . . . when we got in, everybody flocked around for to try an' find out who it was that got lost an' what happened.

Well now, you take Sable Island . . . that's the graveyard of the Atlantic . . . that's what they call it. The island's 'bout fifty miles long in all – an' not'in' but sand. It's a nice place to fish around when it's fine, but you want to know what you're doin' when it's rough. Oh, there was lots o' fish there. But there's quite a bend to the island. I don't know just how much bend is into the island – there's a lot, quite a lot – curves around like the new moon, you. An' then on either end there's sand bars . . . them bars run off 'bout fourteen, fifteen miles . . . on either end. An' on the nort' side the water runs deep right to the sand . . . the sand runs down pretty sharp. But on the inside o' the bend it was all belts o' sand. The sea would break on the one belt an' then would ca'm down an' then break on the next one. I t'ink there's about – if I can tell you right – two or t'ree that the sea breaks on.

Vessels'd be fishin' inside that bend an' a southerly wind'd come up an' first t'ing . . . they'd be in a hard fix. You take a sailin' vessel . . . if you got caught there in the bend, well there was lots o' vessels that maybe could work out, but there was lots o' vessels that maybe couldn't work out. If there had o' been power in them days . . .

well, there wouldn't o' been so many vessels smashed up there. Would o' been a different story, you. I never heard tell of any boat that got ashore gettin' off . . . get into shoal water wit' the wind pushin' you onto the island, well, you might as well say that was your end. When it's rough it's all breakin' seas . . . you could hear 'em roar . . . just roar.

We was anchored one night – fishin' wit' Wilson Walters – anchored inside the nor'west bar an' a gale come up, you. Right sudden. An' we had to make it across the bar or go ashore . . . so we put all sail on. Every sail we had to put on, we put on, you. An' we sailed acrost the bar . . . an' when we got acrost to the other side, the sand layed on the deck. That's how close we came to bein' gone . . . sand was all o'er the deck. If the vessel didn't lay o'er, she wouldn't o' went acrost . . . she would o' struck, you. I don't know how much water was under her but she must o' dragged right o'er. It blowed . . . put all sail on an' let 'er go . . . an' she layed right o'er.

You've got to make it one way or the other. If we didn't make it acrost . . . we was, I guess, lucky.

I say it would be hard to believe that a man could . . . could ever . . . ever survive some o' them things that happened. I heard my father tell of one time that they was fishin' around Sable Island. An' they wasn't far from the bar when they was fishin'. An' my father an' Silas Himmelman were dory mates. They were down to the leeward an' the first t'ing it breezed up an' the trawl parted. And in them times there was nothin' like power . . . it was hard goin'.

They was there an' they only had one choice to make . . . keep rowin' or go ashore on the bar. If they got on the bar they was gone. An' the bar wasn't a mile astern of 'em. They could see the breakers on the bar an' the vessel was up ahead . . . of the wind. They rowed an' they rowed. An' I heard my father say not once but a dozen times that the man he had with him was two or t'ree times goin' to call it quits. An' Father, he used to say, "No. Hang to it. Hang to it."

After a while they got up . . . they made the vessel. And when they took their hands off the oars they were painted red wit' blood. From pullin' so long onto it . . . blood come t'rough their hands. Wonderful now, ain't it . . . what a man can go t'rough.

We was on a summer trip down off of Sable Island. An' this day it was rough – the wind was breezin' up all the time. Well, we was all rigged up, had the bait all out in the buckets. Layin' 'round to see if we was goin' to get out. The second hand that would call us out was layin' there wit' oil clothes on in the bunk. All hands had oil clothes on in case we got called out. The vessel, she started to go into it – the seas – an' we didn't t'ink we'd get off.

First t'ing, the second hand come down the companionway, "Dories out!" We come up on deck. Why, it was blowin' half a gale o' wind. I don't know what was the matter that day. We . . . none of us should o' gone. Should o' said, "No, we're not goin' out. We know when it's fit to go." She was rollin' then quite a little bit – an' our bowsprit was commencin' to go down. That's a bad spot . . . if there's any sea runnin', why it just piles up an' breaks – one breaker after anot'er. I couldn't figure goin' out in that weather. The Cap'n, he was a good skipper. I liked 'im. Cared about his men – not like some. You see, when he got the men out, an' it got rough, then he got all worked up, t'inkin' maybe some o' the men would get drowned or somethin'. But the second hand told us to go out an' we went out.

I said to myself, "I won't be goin' very far from the vessel today. Whoever wants to go far can go, but I won't be goin'. I'll buck up ahead, ahead of the cable an' clear the vessel an' fire the anchor o'erboard." But I bucked a little farther than that. An' I kept an eye on the vessel – she was pitchin' somethin' heavy in the seas. Her bowsprit was startin' to go down. Anyway, I anchored. An' I got my lines o'er which I should o' never put 'em over a'tall, 'cause it was only craziness. So anyway, I t'ink I had just a couple o' fish. An' the first t'ing I seen the sign. See they hoisted a flag up on the mainmast. Well that meant come aboard.

Well, I got my anchor up. I'll tell you it was right rough. When the vessel come down, her bowsprit went right under. An' it was one rail in an' one rail out – that's how dirty it was. So I got alongside. I got the dory straightened up 'cause I only had – I didn't have no fish to speak of. I fired my painter up an' the t'roater, he grabbed it. An' boys the vessel rolled, an' when she took the roll, instead of him slackin' the painter off – left her to go down with the vessel – he snugged her. Tried to hold the dory 'gainst the roll, see. An' I went down between the vessel an' the dory – an' the dory struck me. Well, when the vessel come back, Norman Wagner – poor feller is dead an' buried now – he grabbed me an' got me up. He says, "Go down for'ard – you're hurt." Well, when I got my senses back I wasn't very well pleased – a feller could o' been hurt real bad. That was my part into it.

An' after I got aboard I come to find out we got one dory missin'. Well, that ain't a good feelin' to have a feller out in a storm like that. Anot'er feller, he went up . . . up on the topmast – to the crosstrees. An' I t'ink he was up there pretty near three hours . . . lookin' for him. Next thing he hollered down to the old man. He said, "Cap'n, I believe I see a dory."

He said, "No!"

"Yes, I believe I do. Haul 'er up to the sou'west." Well the Cap'n, he did that . . . an' this feller hollered down, "Yes. He's paddlin' – looks like he's paddlin' wit' a bulk headin'." Then he aimed her right fair for him. An' then he sent four dories after 'im. We thought he was gone . . . but we got him.

Filled his dory . . . seas broke o'er the dory an' filled 'er. He lost everyt'in' he had into her . . . his sail, his oars. All he had left was a bulk headin'. An' he was layin' o'er the bow pushin' that way wit' the bulk headin' . . . his dory all awash. That's the way he saved himself.

An' like I told you, the skipper, he got kind o' worked up when he was into a tight spot. He used to smoke a pipe an' he used to chew tobacco. Well, I want to tell you the tobacco spit was flyin' that day.

⚓

Well, we started out the spring of 1922 on the frozen baitin' an' I went second hand wit' Cap'n Angus Walters on the *Bluenose* – the year after she was built. I looked at the cable he took aboard an' I told him that it wasn't a very good lookin' cable for to go on the frozen baitin'. He says, "That's a new cable."

I said, "Hell, all right."

So we went out . . . an' we got in a hurricane off the sou'west bar on Sable Island an' first t'ing the anchor was off – cable parted. The vessel was adrift an' blowin' toward the island. Angus said we should try to heave the cable in. Well, we was heavin'-hovin' a little while an' I said there wasn't much sense in that because we had to condemn the cable anyway. So I went back an' told him, I said, "Why not cut that cable off? I just seen an outside trawl buoy go up past this side. That's one mile from where we was anchored. We're driftin' in here pretty fast." An' I said, "Damn it we're goin' down there pretty fast."

"By t'under," he said, "I wouldn't like to lose all that cable." You see, the cable parted right down close to the anchor. That's what made that a bad t'ing.

I said, "I wouldn't give two cents for that cable. Cut the damn t'ing off. Cut it," I said.

He said, "How much cable did you heave in yet?"

"Not too much," I said. "We should cut it."

"No. Make it if you can."

So I said, "We can, we can get it in for all that, we can. But we should've chopped it long ago." A bad sea was on an' I was scared it would take someone o'erboard, you know, o'er the side. It was howlin' like a bull, the wind. It was howlin', I could hear it howlin' t'rough the riggin' an' everywheres.

Well we was heavin' that damn old t'ing in an' all the time it was breezin' up. We finally heaved in the rest of it, what was left. I didn't t'ink much of the situation, I'll tell you that. After a while I went back to him again. "The wind's haulin'," he said.

"Well," I said, "how's the wind haulin', old man?"

"North to nor'west."

"Well," I said, "that's haulin' in our favour. All you have to do is veer the vessel an' go the other way."

"Take the lead ahead an' have a sound," he says. I took the lead ahead an' sounded. It was eleven fat'om. We was gettin' in closer. I could see the sand in the water then . . . the water was right white wit' sand. I went back an' I looked at the compass. Sizin' up the situation, you understand. I seen she was headed right into the nor'west. I told him again, I said, "Why don't you veer the vessel 'round an' let 'er go down the other way, down past the island? You're not goin' to get acrost the bar because the wind is haulin' that way. That's the way it's startin' to haul an' that's the way it's goin' to finish up an' you can't make it."

He said, "You t'ink we can veer her?"

I said, "Do you t'ink we can veer her! Why not? Either veer her or let her tear herself to pieces. One or the other. It's just as bad as that."

"All right," he said. "Stand by." And he swung 'er off. I'd say that vessel went two miles. She went off to the side o' the wind . . . down . . . around. With the sea heavin' in there on the island . . . she done good. She headed up almost to the sou'east. It was the only t'ing we could do.

Alby, my brother, was wit' us. It was bein' his watch, first watch. An' he said, "Don't keep us too full."

I said, "Hoist the jumbo so we can get a little headway onto 'er." I felt good then because I knowed we was clear of the island.

"Oh, I don't t'ink," he said.

"Yes," I said, "hoist the jumbo yet." Forestaysail is the right name of it, but we called it the jumbo. An' we hoisted it. Then we had the fores'l, stormsail, an' jumbo on.

An' he said, "Don't keep 'er too full."

"You go down below an' we'll watch 'er." First t'ing, I seen the water come o'er an' right down the stairs to the companionway an' strike my brother. He come up – soakin' wet – an' said, "You're keepin' 'er too full."

Well, she took a couple of old wallows while she was goin' off. But she done famous . . . she done famous. An' she never drifted off any, you know. She held her own, see. That's the beauty of it. I knowed she could do it.

When we were off an' our watch was up, I said to Alby, "You get the lead tub an' I'll take the lead ahead." Well, I took the lead ahead, like you would to the foreriggin' for to t'row it o'erboard tryin' to get a plumb sound, you know. An' a sea broke. I heard it – couldn't see . . . it was dark. I heard the sea roarin'. An' I sung out to Alby, "Watch out, there's a sea comin'!" An' I jumped for the riggin' an' I lost the riggin'. An' the next t'ing it picked me up . . . I was goin' o'er the cabin there . . . an' all kinds o' bait boards we had – big planked bait boards. The sea tore them right off. It was me an' the bait boards goin' t'rough the sling lift on the main gaff. The bait boards went t'rough, but I caught the sling lift on the main gaff. When she was up – come up out o' the water, the water run off her – I called to Alby, "Alby, are you all right?"

"Am I all right! Am I all right! You got too damn much sail onto her!" He was down in the cabin. He'd jumped down into the companionway. He was safe enough. See, that's all I was feared of – was him . . . that he was gone. We got the lead cleared out of the mess an' took it up an' sounded. We had thirty fat'om o' water, thirty fat'om. We were out o'er the edge, startin' to get out o'er the edge o' the bar. That was around two o'clock in the night.

An' then, toward mornin', there was a sea struck us before mornin'. I don't know when it struck 'er . . . but it woke 'bout everybody up. Struck 'er for'ard . . . smashed the rail all off. Tore everythin' off her from the bowsprit right back to the break beam. Cleaned 'er right off, you. When daylight come, then we had to look for gear. An' we got all o' the gear back – about all. But that old rotten cable – we still had that.

Bent anot'er anchor onto it an' t'rowed it o'erboard. An' there come a little blow again. First t'ing, the anchor was off again. Then we lost a set o' gear that time. Lost a set o' gear . . . the whole damn works . . . two seas o'er the deck an' it was gone. An' still we hove that cable in. Had to go to Lunenburg then – we had no gear, you see. Went to Lunenburg an' got fixed up – got the damage fixed an' a new set o' gear. We was there a week or so, there till we got straightened up.

Well, we condemned that cable – it wasn't no good an' I knowed it. I told the old man that – but no, he wouldn't listen. That damn t'ing got us in a nasty old mess, but the *Bluenose*, she done famous. She pulled us out, you . . . an' I was onto plenty o' vessels that couldn't'a done what she done. She done good . . . she done famous, you.

The first vessel I was in I was wit' Cap'n George Himmelman – I was wit' him for eighteen years. The one year then in January of 1941 we was fishin' out o' Halifax in the *Lila B. Boutillier.* We went out in Emerald Bank for to set out fishin', you know. An' when we got out there, we set out two o'clock in the night wit' torches – twelve dories, twenty-four men. An' it came down a snowstorm an' the Cap'n he changed ends an' I didn't know it, an' I got astray in the snowstorm. An' it started to get real dirty then – real nasty, pretty heavy seas runnin'. An' anyway, me an' my dory mate got astray . . . an' we kept astray, like the feller said. They looked for us an' they couldn't find us. An' after a while they left for Halifax.

I said to my dory mate, "Ernie Mossman's vessel lays in there about four miles to the nor'ard of us. I t'ink I'll try to see if I can make him." But when I went there he was gone to Halifax too. I missed him an' I missed Clarence Knickle in the *Theresa O'Conner* an' I missed Forster Corkum. They was all gone in . . . I missed 'em all.

I was driftin' around for nine days . . . for nine days I was driftin' around the ocean. An' I had nothin' to eat. Twenty-eighth day of January . . . every drop o' water froze of ice. We had a fair load o' fish but when we went astray I t'rowed 'em all o'erboard except for two haddock.

So anyway – Wednesday night, seven days gone, it was blowin' hard. Right dark . . . an' long nights . . . short days. I said to my dory mate – I hollered to 'im – I couldn't see 'im. He was in the bow of the dory. I said, "John, I t'ink tomorrow mornin' we'll get picked up." An' boys it was only about an hour after that a sea struck the side o' the dory – it cracked like a pistol. And John went o'erboard. An' he went right under the dory. I grabbed him by the back o' the neck . . . by his oilskins. An' I hauled 'im in.

When he went o'erboard he had a pair of paddles rowin' for to keep the dory so she wouldn't get side to it. An' I had two in the aft for to keep 'er bow to. An' when he went o'erboard, you understand, he lost a pair o' paddles. An' when I jumped for to get 'im, I lost my two. So I couldn't row . . . I had nothin' to row wit'. I just had to set there an' take the whole works. The dory was about – I won't say she was half full o' water – but she had a good junk into 'er. Pretty near to the risens.

John, he flopped himself right down into the water. I took my compass bucket for to bail an' I freed her. I saved her . . . got her free o' water.

That night then . . . pretty cold . . . I said to my dory mate, "How you feelin', John?"

He said, "I'm gettin' cold. I'm cold, Frank."

Well, I said, "I t'ink tomorrow we'll get picked up." That was in my mind all the time. So about twelve or one or two o'clock at night I hollered to John again. I said, "John, how you feelin'?"

He said, "I'm gettin' warmer."

Little did I t'ink he was dyin'. I didn't know it. I t'ought his clothes was dryin' on 'im an' he was gettin' warmer.

The next mornin' just about dawn – you could just about see a person, like a shadow – anot'er sea struck 'er. John went o'erboard. An' he was froze, he must have been froze just the same as a rock. I looked o'er my shoulder . . . well, I seen him go as far as I could look. An' that was all there was to it.

After that I said, "I'll tie myself fast. If somethin' does happen that I die an' they pick up the dory, I'll be tied fast." That's what I said to myself. So that night about – I don't know rightly but to tell you trut'ful it was around eight or nine or ten o'clock – I tied a rope around myself an' to where we tie the sheets to the dory. It was dirty then, black an' ugly, an' I knowed I was goin' to have anot'er snowstorm . . . anot'er dirty time of it.

Well boys, I looked down o'er my left shoulder an' here was a light. About as bright as an electric light – it was no different. An' I kept watchin' at that. I said to myself . . . it was around war time you see . . . right in war time. I t'ought it might be airplanes or submarines . . . somethin' like that. An' that blazin' light come up, you, right up to the dory. Well it was so close I reached my left hand out to see if I could touch it. An' I hollered all I could holler. No answer. An' it left the left hand side o' the dory an' it went around the bow an' it stopped on my right hand side. An' I done the same – I hollered. An' no answer. But it seemed like . . . but the light I'm sure of . . . nobody'll take that away from me, not till I go to my grave. That I seen – an' it seemed like there was somethin' in the bow o' that dory. And I heard it like a noise. An' it seemed like it answered me back. I don't know if . . . it couldn't have been my ears. "Tomorrow mornin', Frank, you're goin' to be picked up." Just like that.

The next mornin' when it was daylight I couldn't see nothin' – I was pretty well blooded up you know. An' by God Almighty that Friday mornin' half past eight I was aboard the trawler *Breaker* out o' Boston. It was ugly weat'er then, blowin' hard. The Cap'n said he changed his course – didn't know what made 'im do it – an' he seen me. An' by God I survived an' got picked up. He put a rope around one of his men an' he went down an' put a rope around me an' hauled the two of us up an' left the dory go. Took me into Boston. An' I spent thirteen months in the hospital. When I got my health back they shipped me from there down to Halifax.

After that I went back wit' the same man, Cap'n George Himmelman. Two years more I was wit' him. Then we got into Halifax one day – dischargin' the cargo – taking' out fish. I was happy as a lark – made about fifty or seventy-five dollars – I can't remember no more. In the wintertime it was. He was walkin' there on the deck. Always wore a pair o' Redjacks – leather boots. An' I never had no intention of anyt'ing you know . . . what I was goin' to hear that day. So he called. He said, "Frank, come back here. I want you."

"Well," I said to myself, "what does he want?"

"Frank," he said, "I got news for you." He talked right rough – a good natured man – but he talked right rough. An' I looked at 'im – it was right by the wheel house. "I'm not goin' to take you no more. An' don't you go wit' nobody else neither."

"Why," I said, "old man?"

"Well," he said, "it hurts my heart for what you went t'rough. I'm not dumpin' you o'er the rail no more." He told me in there on the wharf in Lunenburg several times after that, he said, "I hated to tell you 'cause you was a good man but I hadn't the conscience to put you into a dory no more. 'Cause for what you went t'rough I didn't know if you'd ever get back or not."

See, it got to him so that he wouldn't take me no more. An' then next spring I was wit' . . . wit' anot'er feller . . . went out on the spring trip, you. An' after that I was wit' Cap'n Leo Lohnes in the *Douglas Mosher* an' then wit' Cap'n Arnold Parks in the *Ocean Maid.* Like the feller said, I kept at it . . . kept at it for a good many years.

Well, we were fishin' in a little vessel called the *Sea Rover*. An' there was seven of us on 'er. We had a little trip, not a real big one, but we had some fish. It was t'ree days before Christmas when we left for to come down. Blowin' a nice little breeze, but fine clear weather . . . it was blowin', I would say about fifty mile o' wind. She done time, was makin', I'd say, 'bout eleven, twelve knots an hour. An' we'd had a little storm about two weeks before that an' the jumbo was blowed away . . . but the halyard was still there yet . . . which was a Godsend.

So, I was on watch, an' come time for me to go off. An' this feller that come to relieve me – he was a nice feller, a good shipmate – but if he seen a light twenty-five times a day, an' then the next week from that . . . it would be just a light to him. Didn't make no impression, you understand. So I said to him, "Now," I said, "when we get down to Little Gull Light, then call the old man." See, when you got down to Little Gull, then you changed course. So that's the reason I wanted him to call the Cap'n. I give him the course an' I went down an' I turned in.

An', Jesus, I don't know . . . I might of been in about an hour, an hour an' a half, an' first t'ing – Bango! She hit. Well, all I could t'ink of was that a steamer had rammed us because, you know, it was as clear a night as the Lord ever could let shine. But it blowed a gale o' wind . . . a lot o' wind. I can remember when she hit I jumped – not only me, but everybody that was in the fo'c's'le. An' I run for the deck t'inkin' to see a steamer or somethin' in 'er side. An' when I looked up, all I could see was a high clift. An' if we struck two hundred feet farther down, would of never been a man left to tell the tale 'cause there was no way in the world to get off 'cause we'd'a went right slam bang up against the side o' the clift, an' that was it. But the way we were, where we hit was a high clift all right – but there was about fifty or seventy-five feet o' sand from the clift off, y'know. So she piled up on the sand before she could get a chance to hit the clift. We run onto the shore like on an angle, see, an' that made like a funnel.

Well, the first sea that struck 'er come in o'er the stern an' it smashed in the cabin house doors aft. Well, the old man's first words were, "Get the dories. Put the dories o'erboard!"

An' I'll never forget my words. I said, "If I can lose my life here tonight, it's not goin' to be back there." The dories, you understand, was on top o' the house – on the stern. They went back for to try to see what they could do . . . got the first one down an' before that got in the water, that was smashed up like a match box. An' the first t'ing, the next sea come. We didn't get a chance to get t'other one down. She took that one. Well that was it. There we were . . . heavy sea goin' an' not a dry place for us – about I'd say fifteen, twenty feet from the sand bank. An' then the sea was breakin' o'er her stern. It would go right around 'er bow, y'know. An' we had our fores'l on yet an' when the sea would hit 'er, it would t'row 'er in, an' when the water run out, she'd go t'other way. She was just like on a swing . . . on a swing.

So . . . what are we goin' to do? I said, "Well, I'll tell you what I'm goin' to do. I'm goin' ashore on that halyard" – jumbo halyard like I was tellin' you. "If I can get ashore, I'm goin' to take the chance." So I got a'hold o' this halyard. An' I stood on the port side . . . on the rail. An' when she listed off like that – that would be away from the beach – I got onto the rail wit' this t'ing, an' I held onto it. An' when the next sea hit 'er, when she started to go towards the beach, then I said, "Here she goes." An' I left 'er go. I swung on off the rail. I hung onto it till I figured that I was as far as I was goin' to get – an' I let go. When I let go, my two feet struck the sand an' I was in the water up to my middle. An' at that time o' year, it wasn't none the warmest – two days before Christmas. But . . . in them conditions, that didn't bother you. It was just a matter of . . . life or death.

Anyway, when she rolled back, the halyard an' tackle come back. An' one o' the fellers hollered, "There's a buoy ashore somewhere." See, at the time I didn't know it, but Eddie Cornell, he'd run back an' t'rowed one of our marker buoys o'er wit' a coil o' rope tied onto it – had t'other end fastened aboard the boat. First t'ing I got snarled up in this moorin' line. An' I kept pullin' an' by an' by, she set tight. An' there was a big granite rock about eight, ten feet from the high clifts. An' I went up an' wound five, six turns around that rock. See the distance wasn't so far . . . it was far enough wit'out the help o' somethin' to hold on to . . . there was no way that you could keep on your feet wit'out holdin' onto somethin'. An' I took a'hold o' this rope an' . . . well, wit' the rope, I could get off, I'd say within' ten or twelve feet from the boat. But the minute a sea would come, why my two feet would just go out from under me . . . Well, first t'ing, they sung out, "Landry is comin'." He was a big man an' when he fell, he fell! But he didn't hit the sand – he hit the water. It was dark – nighttime – but anyway I got a'hold of 'im an' got 'im on his feet. Now I don't want to get the praise of it all, but I was the first man ashore to take care of what come next. Well, Landry got a'hold of the moorin' line an' that's the way they come . . . one after t'other. An' the only feller that wouldn't take the halyard to come ashore . . . he was the man that had the wheel. An' he was as far in the bow as he could get, bawlin' like a bull . . . hollerin' an' screechin' his head off. Everybody tellin' him, "Take the halyard an' come ashore." But there was no way. An' the first t'ing, there was one sea hit 'er an' it brought 'er up . . . you could o' walked onto 'er wit' hip boots on – brought 'er up right high an' dry. Then he didn't have to take the jump – he could walk ashore.

So the next t'ing – Where are we? What are we goin' to do? I said to Fred Landry, "Fred, let's see if we can get up on top o' this clift." So we went that way an' anot'er bunch went the ot'er way. Well, if it would'a been daylight, it would'a been no problem, but it was five or six in the mornin'. An' it was all woods . . . we was feelin' our way t'rough. An' by an' by I got to a heap o' cow manure an' I said, "By God, Fred, faith has delivered us! There's got to be somebody handy here or that wouldn't be here." So, we kept goin' along an' we didn't go very fast – wet an' half cold. An' by an' by we broke t'rough the edge o' the woods an' I said, "There's a light, Fred. Good enough." So we goes up to the door – an' this was six o'clock in the mornin' – an' knocks. An' the man come out.

He says, "What do you want?" Well, if you open the door an' see two big fellers like us standin' there an' soakin' wet an' dirty an' one t'ing an' anot'er . . . I suppose we didn't look real happy to him. He off an' hauled the door shut in our face an' shut the outside light off.

An' I said to Fred, I says, "Fred, that don't look so good y'know."

Fred said, "We'll stay here till daylight." He says, "We can stick it out till daylight an' then we'll get fixed up." An' we stood there for about five minutes.

First t'ing, the door opened an' he said, "Come in." We walks in, me an' Fred. An' when we got in the house, there was t'ree more men besides himself. There was

H

four . . . he had t'ree sons. An' he was a feller by the name o' Prince, an' he sure was a prince. A nicer man you couldn't of ever wished to meet. But before he'd leave us in, he went upstairs an' he got his t'ree sons out'a bed – for to know that he was on the best side o' the battle. Anyway, after we got the rest o' the fellers, we had our breakfast an' I'll never forget what we had – was bacon an' eggs which was lovely. Well, we got fixed up – dry clothes an everythin'. An' I t'ink it was the day after Christmas that we got home. Messed up Christmas a little, you.

My father was drowned seventy odd year ago . . . I was only four years old. He was drowned on the LaHave Banks . . . three brothers . . . at one time. They was in a vessel, a small vessel. Well, the one dory parted . . . I don't know if I can tell you right – I can only tell you as I heard it. One dory parted . . . an' they went down to get the dory an' my father put two of his brothers in the one dory an' he pulled back to the vessel. An' they got part o' the way up an' a sea struck 'em an' turned the dory o'er . . . an' Dad, he went back down to get 'em again. He had, I t'ink, the one feller in the dory but . . . well, he was about played out . . . he couldn't make it. An' the sea turned that dory o'er too. One o' his other brothers, Clarence, an' William Bush was in the vessel . . . they brought her in. I just about can remember . . . when the vessel come in. Four years old I was . . . I just about can remember the vessel comin' in up there in what they call the Cape Channel. It was a sad time . . . . It was. I was four years old . . . my father an' his two brothers . . . John an' Norman. It was a hard t'ing. Will Bush said Clarence wanted to jump o'erboard . . . wanted to make away wit' himself . . . that's what he said. That's about all I can remember from that. My uncle up here, Wells Wamboldt, I guess could tell you more on that.

I had t'ree brothers drowned at one time off here. I was only nine year old at the time. My t'ree brothers got gone. Seventy-four years the twenty-sixth of this June comin' that they were lost.

Well, they had a small vessel . . . there was four brothers onto 'er, an' anot'er feller, Will Bush. But the one brother, he got saved. Small vessel – her name was *Iselda*. Two dories they had, an' they had their dories hangin' astern an' a gale o' wind hit 'er. An' this one dory parted from the stern, you know, an' went adrift. My t'ree brothers went after the dory an' when they was rowin' back, the seas capsized 'em. The t'ree of 'em got lost. They said one feller had a sprained wrist I guess in the one dory. That caused the trouble altogether. Most of it.

Why, it's no use to go there an' lose your life on account o' some gear an' stuff like that. It's better to let it go. The Devil wit' it. You can make up for gear. That's why I say my brothers should o' left that damn old dory go. Could o' got anot'er dory but . . . my brothers . . . . An' that's what happened there. Two dories gone . . . an' t'ree men was gone.

It was five fellers aboard – four Wamboldt brothers an' my grandmother's second husband, William Bush. We used to call him Gran'pa Billy. Well, the t'ree fellers that got lost was brothers . . . John, Norman, an' Will. They were brave men, you – them Wamboldts. You see the way they got lost, the dory – the painter o' the dory broke free o' the vessel. An' Will Wamboldt, he started to cry out, "I can't lose the dory. Can't lose the dory."

William Bush said, "Don't go for the dory. You'll never get back."

But Will was set on it, see. He says, "I can't lose the dory. John, go wit' me." So they got out in a dory – John an' Norman an' Will Wamboldt . . . headed down for to pick up the stray dory. Will got aboard the vessel wit' his dory, but John an' Norman that was in the dory they went after didn't get aboard 'cause John, he had a bad wrist – an' they couldn't row up against the wind. An' when they seen that they couldn't get aboard, Will – he was the skipper – he said, "I'm goin' back for to help 'em." An' before he got to 'em . . . well, the seas broke o'er the dories . . . they was bottom up. Two fellers was on each side o' the one dory wit' their arms holdin' fast to one anot'er's hands . . . across the bottom of one dory. The other one – that was Will's – drifted away. That was the last they seen of 'em. See, it was the storm that broke the painter off the dory, but it wasn't the storm that took 'em. It was their own fault. They went after the dory an' it wasn't fit to go.

William Bush, he brought the vessel in – he was older than the rest. Clarence wanted to jump o'erboard 'cause they couldn't save 'em, see. Bill, he locked him down, he locked the door in the fo'c's'le . . . wouldn't let him up 'cause he'd'a went o'erboard – so broke up see. Came in wit' the flag at half-mast. Oh it was a sad thing.

Twenty-sixth of June. Clarence, I guess, he never spoke a word all summer. He used to come where we were . . . we was all about the same age, but you couldn't get 'im to talk. He wouldn't talk. Just set wit' his head down, t'inkin' about it.

We seen the boat come in. William Bush an' Clarence Wamboldt was aboard her . . . they brought the boat in. We didn't know till they come . . . when we seen the flag half-mast. Then we knowed somebody was gone. Didn't know who was left until they got in. Well, when they got in, there was a lot o' sadness . . . an' cryin'. Will was married to the woman that lived right o'er here . . . she was my cousin. Left two young children . . . Harold an' Amy. John was single an' Norman was single. Norman was twenty. That was a hard slap for the island. A hard slap.

There used to be a lot o' men lost on them vessels. A vessel went trawlin' . . . sometimes they'd lose a couple o' men every summer. You didn't know who was goin' to be lost till the vessel got back home. See, they had no way to send any word in them times like they have today wit' them ship to shore radios. I seen a good many vessels come in here wit' their flags at half-mast. That wasn't a very good t'ing to see, you. The wharf was crowded wit' people, right crowded wit' people. All the families. They seen the flag down, you understand, an' they knowed someone was gone. But they didn't know who it was.

Oh it's sad . . . yes sad. Way back when I was a boy, there was no compensation or nothin' for to help the widow out. There was nothin' like that for to get. Now just how widows got along . . . I can't tell you that. A lot o' women lost their men in them days . . . there was a church service in the fall o' the year. They had a church service every fall for the men from out around here that was lost at sea. Every year . . . there was somebody . . . always men lost.

# You Was a Millionaire

I always say people in them times was a lot happier than they are today. Sure. They didn't have so much . . . they didn't have what the people have today, but they didn't look for it either. You couldn't get the t'ings if they would'a been available. There wasn't as much money, but everybody seemed so happy. People did t'ings an' lived different an' mixed wit' one anot'er an' everybody was good friends. And now the world's divided like. There don't seem to be the same kind o' friends. Too much money. One person don't care for t'other. I remember back . . . there was nice feelin's in them times.

Everythin' is so changed. Why out there on the islands there where I was born . . . it's only a few people livin' out there any more . . . an' most o' them is gettin' on in years. It's only . . . the ones that is left . . . I can name 'em off. The rest . . . they're all dead. All dead. People at one time they lived there . . . in the family house . . . until they died. Now the younger ones . . . a good part o' them goes off . . . is gone off somewheres.

Well there's a lot o' people gone from around here. You don't know what homes was out here years ago! Gone. An' when I was young, why everyone had to kind o' work toget'er . . . that's how you got along, see. When the house burnt down up here – it was in the wintertime – men came. They weren't hired – they just came to help an' they went right into the woods an' they cut logs an' they hewed the logs out. They hewed the logs out – the frame o' the house – by hand. Broad axe an' axes. In, I'd say, about t'ree months after the house burnt down they had the frame up . . . an' all done by hand. Hewed it. Men from the community here all joined in to help – everybody came to help. Did it for nothin'. Yes sir. Nowadays, they want eight or nine dollars an hour.

No sir, t'ings aren't the same! It's some sad, you, to see the younger people leave. There's a lot o' places sold to summer people – an' that makes it lonely in the winter – an' there's a lot o' homes left to fall in an' rot. The people that is around . . . well, they seem more off to themselves than what people used to be . . . everybody is for theirselves.

I was just t'inkin' of that picture of Dad I showed you. He was forty-two when he was drowned an' he's been gone for fifty-one year. If he would come back, if he was here now . . . an' seen what was goin' on now . . . he wouldn't believe this is the same place he left. It's nothin' today like it was then.

An' I heard – now, this was before my time – but my grandfather's time . . . the families, they'd leave Kingsburg an' walk to Lunenburg, which would be about twelve miles. Twelve miles an' they'd walk . . . to church. They was awful good church people . . . good church goers. An' walk that distance. An' if they had a pair o' shoes that they thought a lot of, they was taken off, an' they'd give it to 'er barefooted o'er them dirt roads till they got in an' then they'd put their shoes on . . . they'd put their shoes on when they got there. Used to go to church . . . meet people. It was nice.

Up here . . . the church up here would be packed full o' people. Be just an hour service. You go in at seven o'clock – you're out at eight o'clock. Well it'd be nice an' light yet. We'd walk to Crescent Beach – a bunch of us young fellers – an' wherever was a house that had an organ . . . there we'd make for. An' we'd go in there an' sing till ten, eleven o'clock, an' they'd probably serve us a cup o' tea or a little lunch, n' then we'd go home. We did that a good many nights. The young fellers. But get the young fellers today . . . they won't do that. They'd rather go out in a car – sit down in a car – go drivin' somewhere or somethin'. If the young people would do what the old people did years ago, I t'ink it would be a great wonderful t'ing for this community.

Then there was only one way to get visitin' for to have company. You either had to walk or it was stay home. Why, you didn't t'ink not'in' o' walkin' five or six mile an' comin' back home the same evenin'. All dirt roads.

An' in the winter! Sometimes it would take you, I'd say as high as t'ree days to get the roads open after a big snowstorm. There was no snowploughs. We was the ploughs! Everyt'in' was done wit' a shovel. In the fall o' the year, you see, you were sworn in as a road overseer. Now, on a big snowstorm you had to get out an' you had your district to go in – perhaps a mile'd be your section. An' everybody that lives on that section, you'd come to the house say at nine o'clock for shovelin' snow. An' then, from there on, the next overseer'd do it – would warn his men out an' that's the way you'd get the roads open an' the ox teams could go.

It's hard to believe . . . look, when you t'ink back how the world has changed from what it used to be. It's hard to believe . . . at that time, all the people bunched toget'er somehow, somewhere or anot'er, an' had a little party or surprise party or somethin'. Got toget'er, y'know, for a visit. Card party, mat hookin' party an' a wood party . . . whatever, it was a party. But today isn't – people don't . . . mix up. What I mean is, they all got cars, an' they want to go somewheres, they go off. An' them times there was no cars. Makes you feel kind o' sad to t'ink about it . . . the way t'ings have changed. Everyt'ing is easier nowadays an' the people are the worse off for it.

You'd t'ink not'in' o' leavin' Kingsburg an' walkin' to Feltzen South – that's about seven, eight miles – to a dance. T'ink not'in' a'tall of it in the wintertime. An' if the roads was real bad, there used to be an old feller – Willy Wentzel – o'er there that had a big black horse. Hire him – bob sleighs an' wagons full o' straw. An' you'd pile in an' away you'd sail for Feltzen South.

Some o' them fellers o'er in Feltzen South, they used to be as jealous as old sin. You went o'er there an' God, it'd be sometimes hard to get a girl o'er there 'cause their boy friends used to be so jealous they didn't want you to dance wit' 'em. But we most generally . . . well there used to be about twelve, fifteen of us from Kingsburg an' we always had about that many girls to go o'er wit' an' we'd never be stuck. But we used to do a lot o' tantalizin' – takin' their girls an' havin' a dance wit' 'em.

Pie sales o'er there too, an' every girl'd bake a pie an' they'd auction 'em off. Sometimes you'd bunch up, see if . . . say a feller was goin' wit' such an' such a girl an' you had somebody that could point out her pie, then you'd bunch up – about t'ree or four fellers, an' keep drivin' the price up. He'd bid on her pie – two dollars an' sometimes put anot'er dollar on, t'ree . . . sometimes I seen 'em go as high as ten dollars. He'd stick to it that he was goin' to get his girl's pie. An' I remember one time we was goin' soon to the West Indies an' the feller that was master, Lawrence Zinc – dead now – an' we was o'er to this pie sale . . . few days before the trip. He wasn't married then but he was just about to the church. An' we said, "By God – now he wants his pie an' he's goin' to pay for it." An' we kept drivin' – the whole bunch that was wit' 'im. There was five or six that was wit' 'im on the vessel. Well, we got it up to fifteen, sixteen dollars before we let 'im have it, you know. Then we left 'im alone see. Just fun. An' when it was all o'er he was stuck wit' the price, then we'd split it up, you know, whatever the pie cost – split it up. He was bound that he was goin' to go the limit on the pie. Oh, we used to have lots o' fun. I'll never forget it.

Them big tea meetin's used to make up the money for the church. An' all the church people used to bake the fanciest kind – the best kind o' cakes an' pies . . . cold beef, cheese, pickles. Oh, the best kind! Fill the table full. An' then so much for a ticket to get your supper. Wasn't no more'n twenty-five cents, it wouldn't be. Twenty, twenty-five. Fifteen for the children. An' if you had a girlfriend . . . take 'er an' give 'er supper. You'd buy maybe a couple suppers . . . set down an' eat with' 'em to give money to the church. Oh, that was a barrel o' fun.

An' the pies, they'd have biddin' onto 'em. An' the teacher – always was a teacher, from shore – an' somebody was always goin' wit' 'er. An' they had the pie marked, they had the cake that was hers marked. An' when they t'ought the right cake come up, well the rest o' them would drive it up eight, nine dollars . . . just for a pie.

Then have a big dance then, after – clear away for a dance. Everybody was welcome, made no difference where they come from. They come from the shore an' everywhere. Yes, had the best cake an' dances . . . yarn all about fishin' an' stuff. Plenty o' rum, plenty o' Black Diamond. Some had rum an' they'd get t'ree parts drunk. But never no fightin' – no rough stuff like that, y'know. An' that's the way it went.

I have left home in the evenin' wit' a bunch o' fellers an' walked to Broad Cove to a tea meetin'. That's about six or eight miles. An' I'd go up there, dance all evenin', turn around an' walk home again. An' the next mornin' Dad'd say, "You're tired? Get your axe, come on, we're goin' in the woods." Wouldn't be tired. No.

You take now forty, fifty years ago . . . a family knowed what twenty, thirty dollars was. We maybe didn't have so much but we knowed what we had. Well, I guess that a person now's got too many luxuries. Now it's too much. An' you don't enjoy it 'cause you got too much. I've said that so many times. Too many luxuries . . . an' the younger people don't know how to get along wit'out. Now I'll tell you somethin' . . . you might laugh, but it's as true as I'm settin' here. My parents had no timepiece, an' old Dad there, one day he went to work an' he made a mark there on the window, in that nor'west window there. An' when the sun got around to that mark, why then he imagined that was twelve o'clock. That's right! Told the hours by that . . . couldn't afford to buy a timepiece.

We had no money in them days but we done all right. Kept a pig an' some chickens – kill the pig on the first o' December. You could buy a can o' milk for ten cents, get a pound o' butter for twenty cents an' you could get a bag o' flour for t'ree an' a quarter . . . that's a hundred an' ninety-six pounds. Then we used to plant a little . . . an' that'd help you along that way. In them days you made do . . . .

You live now like we did them times, you'd have some money . . . I never seen forty dollars at one time. Never. A hundred dollars, why that'd be a fortune. A fortune you.

The minister he was boardin' down here in Stonehurst into the house of Mr. Cornelius Gilfoy an' his wife. Well, the minister wanted to get up to Lunenburg an' Mr. Gilfoy he was away. So he asked me if I would go along an' help to paddle the boat. See there was no cars at that time an' there was no ot'er way to get to Lunenburg but to take a skiff an' row up to the back wharf an' walk up town. Well I was only young – I couldn't do much wit' a pair o' those big oars. But we got up anyway. Me an' the minister an' old Mrs. Tanner an' Mrs. Gilfoy.

An' we got up to what they call the back wharf. When we got on the wharf, why the minister come to me an' he said, "You want somethin' to eat m'boy." He gave me two ten-cent pieces. I t'ought that was a lot o' money.

We got up in the town an' it come up toward dinner time. There was an old feller up there by the name o' Johnny Bailey – kept a lunch counter. I was there before – I knew where to go. So I had my dinner there . . . for t'ree cents mind you . . . a cent for a glass o' lime juice an' two cents for the molasses cookies. Got t'ree cookies – they were big ones – round an' pretty t'ick. So I had those down an' the glass o' lime juice. I felt pretty comfortable I can tell you as far as that was concerned.

An' then there was an old feller by the name o' P.H. Ross – kept a general store an' he happened to be my Sunday school teacher right o'er here in the church. An' him an' I – we got along pretty well. Well he had all this little stuff stickin' around there. An' the first t'ing caught my eye was a harmonica . . . ten cents. I bought it. Well, I looked around a little more. There was a Jew's harp there. I forget what that was any more, an' a pistol an' a box o' caps . . . an' I was two cents in the hole. I owed him two cents. An' bein' as I was one of his scholars in Sunday school he liked me pretty well – and he exempted me of the two cents. But it was two cents an' two cents was a lot at that time . . . don't t'ink it wasn't.

All that stuff I bought for my two ten-cent pieces. Yes sir, I was some happy. Today for twenty cents you can buy nothin'. Nothin' a'tall.

We didn't see much store bought stuff back then, you. People knew how to do more for themselves, see. Had to . . . had to make for yourself or go wit'out. Not like today – run up to the stores an' . . . buy this an' that.

The women, they'd grow flax. An' then they'd have a place built – it would be, oh, bigger than this room, an' high – all walled up wit' rock. An' they had stringers across. They'd spread that flax back an' forth onto that. An' make a fire under that – to dry it see. Then they'd get it out, an' they'd have sticks, an' they used to call 'em thrashers – sticks about, oh say, as long as a broom handle an' a little heavier. They'd lay the flax on the barn floor an' they'd pound that an' pound the shell off of it an' then when the shell was off all you'd have was the thread inside. An' that was spun an' wove up – in clothes an' petticoats.

An' I can remember when you wanted a pair o' winter stockin's. You went up to the shop an' there was a reel an' it'd be perhaps eight, ten yards o' stockin' – just the leg part of it. An' you'd say, "I want two feet, four feet." Whatever you needed. The women'd take the legs home an' knit the feet onto it. An' that's how you got your stockin's.

Anot'er t'ing – you wasn't in society if you didn't have a good hay rake an' a spinnin' wheel for to spin wool. Eight, nine women'd get toget'er. They'd have some . . . perhaps they'd have about twenty, thirty sheep an' they'd have a spinnin' party, spin toget'er. Go off to the cardin' mill, have it carded – then they'd sit there an' they'd spin an' gossip.

An' I can remember when I was a boy an' I'd go out wit' my mother in hay makin' time. There was nothin' like tractors – big pairs of oxen wit' big ladders onto the wagons. The men, they'd load on perhaps a ton or so o' somebody's hay. An' two women'd be comin' after them rakin' up the hay. An' when they were t'rough, a swallow wouldn't get enough to make a nest. Everyt'in' was clean. Now they put a match in that to burn it off the ground.

An' today there isn't an animal in the place. Look, in Kingsburg there's one cow today. One cow! An' one time, look – I can remember when I was a boy . . . most every man had a cow an' everyone, everybody had a team. My father always kept – if he didn't have a pair, he'd have a big single ox. You'd go down here on the beach after a storm an' haul that sea manure – kelp – for plantin' in the spring. After a storm you'd go down there an' you'd see fifty, seventy-five pairs of oxen, haulin'. Haulin' kelp. Haulin', haulin', haulin'. That was some sight, you, them oxen stringed out along the beach.

But the world has changed a lot. Livin' has changed, people has changed an' . . . I don't know what it's goin' to be all about. Your livin' come off the land then.

Look, what chances I had to go to school, I didn't have to have any gymnasium for to keep me in shape. I'll tell you where we used to get our shape – on The Grand Banks, fishin'. An' when you come home from that, then you made about five or six, seven hundred quintals o' fish. Each feller took a share out o' the vessel see an' dried 'em – got 'em ready for market. They had to be all washed an' dried on flakes. Put 'em out on the flakes in the cool dry air o' fall. That was your fall's work, to do that.

An' when that was over, then the next was grab your wood axe an' go to the woods to get your winter's wood. My old dad, he had two pieces o' woodland up in back of Indian Path – the one had, I t'ink, seven acres o' wood on it an' the other one, not so big. An' you went up there an' if you cut a tree that was green you was in trouble. You had to go t'rough an' pick out all the dry ones – a green tree couldn't be cut. It had to be dry. You wouldn't cut the green wood, you see, because that'd be part o' your land . . . your property. The dry trees'd be rottin' to waste an' you'd be cuttin' the good ones. Let the good ones grow, see. An' you'd cut all day an' if you found a tree as big around as my leg, well you was lucky. Then you'd haul home about twenty-five, thirty ox loads an' pile her up. First chance then, you'd have a sawin' party. Dad'd call out, "We're havin' a sawin' party." You didn't feel embarrassed 'bout sayin', "Come on up an' help a little." "Sure, I'll be there." Was no sayin', "No, I can't come 'cause I got so much to do" or "I'm goin' somewhere." No. No. "I'll be there." That's the way it would be. An' perhaps you'd have ten, fifteen fellers – the whole gang out. In them times they had them old cross-cut saws an' you'd team up an' saw away. Perhaps have a little hooch or somethin', a bottle o' somethin'. Out to the wood place there'd be twelve, fourteen boys or young men an' in the house there might be eight, ten girls workin' on a mat – havin' a mat party in there. Saw wood by day, then after supper, dance in the night. Have a good time . . . there's nothin' like that any more. Big feed o' beans an' everythin'. It was just . . . happy. You was a millionaire. That's just . . . that's all done away with.

It was quite a change, quite a difference, you. I can remember when we burned all wood. Not'in' but a wood stove. Go to work an' get up here four o'clock in the mornin', an' take your boat – row boat – an' row o'er to Cape LaHave, an' then walk about two mile from one corner o' the Cape acrost to the other side, down the outside part o' the Cape. Cut wood all day, an' then go to work an' walk back again – row home. Stars'd be in the sky.

Well, then we used to sometimes . . . you cut into a bad place where you couldn't get in – we used to have to use hand sleighs for to haul it. But, cut into a place where you couldn't get at it wit' this sleigh – so you might have to carry it maybe, oh, maybe a quarter of a mile on your shoulder, piece by piece. One piece at a time. An' we used to have to do that, carry it till you got it all by the road. An' then, get a bunch o' men toget'er – when the conditions got right you know, snow enough – an' haul the sleigh by hand to the shore. An' then go to work, when you had it to the shore, when spring come an' the ice got away – we used to have dories then, double dories – an' take your dory an' your boat, an' go back an' load your dory an' your boat an' bring it home that way. An' then pile it on the wharf down here where them traps is.

Well then, you had a – a sawin' party – call the fellers out an' saw it all up. An' then it had to be split.

I can remember workin' . . . workin' in the wintertime out here in the moonlight, out here behind the house splittin' wood. Splittin' all that . . . an' I'll tell you, it was a big job . . . but I enjoyed it then. I was young then.

I used to like a good wood fire. A stove, you can get up close to an' get yourself warm. Oh, years ago, look into the winter, we used to have an old wood stove goin' full blast. Look, it was nice. An' you didn't have no heat upstairs, but you went to bed an' got yourself covered up an' you wasn't there long before you was warm. We never used to mind it all that bad. Nowadays, the furnace goin', an' the heat . . . well, it ain't the same. It ain't half as good as it used to be then. I don't like it as well. I used to like it better when I went to bed wit' the cold. You know it's funny when you stop an' t'ink about it but all these conveniences that a person has today, it's not cosy.

I know here when you baked homemade bread wit' the wood fire – it was some good, you! Want to toast a piece o' toast . . . you had one o' these old – you t'row the piece o'bread in an' clamp 'em toget'er, stick 'er on top o' the stove an' toast 'er. An' when you got up by the stove you know you enjoyed the heat.

It was good. I don't know, today's times, I guess they are better, but . . . it was good then.

I'm ninety-three. I can make out workin' around yet. Cut all my wood an' everyt'ing. Cut, an' haul it out, saw it up, an' split it up. I burn forty sleigh loads in a winter. A hand sleigh. I take my time . . . saw it an' split it up. I don't mind sawin' it. I can saw up forty sleigh loads in a short time – few days. But splittin' takes a long time – them big junks. That's what I mind. Splittin' takes me a long time. Takes me a whole month to split it up. Years gone by . . . well, there was others around that would help one anot'er out. T'ings has gotten bad . . . bad times. Bad times, you.

# Made a Trip Down Sout'

I'll tell you how t'ings was around here years ago . . . in times gone by the harbours along the shore here an' up the river, why they was filled wit' boats. See, supplies – some of 'em was brought down from Halifax by rail, but most of 'em were brought down on small coastin' vessels. There was one boat there, the *Emma Cook* – I t'ink she was called – that come down t'rough here every week. Mahone Bay, Chester, Lunenburg, Riverport, an' up to Bridgewater, bringin' supplies – staple goods, paint, dry goods, nails, lard, hundred pound bags o' sugar – that's how you bought your sugar. An' barrels o' flour – two hundred pounds . . . five pound tins o' tea. You name it. All that stuff was brought down on them little schooners . . . an' then she'd take lumber an' shingles an' some fish back into Halifax – they'd take dried cod fish, an' herrin' an' mackerel into some o' the fish firms in Halifax – A.M. Smith was one, an' Pickford an' Black – Robin, Jones an' Whitman I t'ink was anot'er one. A lot o' shippin' just along the coast here.

Then see . . . my God man, we used to go up the river here to Bridgewater . . . an' on both sides o' the river you'd see them big square-rigged ships layin' there. An' there was some big ones! They'd lay out in the harbour waitin' for a sou'east wind to go up – there was no engines into 'em – an' then they'd come down wit' a Nor'wester. Big square-rigged ships . . . they'd be up the river loadin' lumber. Oh, was a lot o' shippin' down out o' here. There'd be – on the railroad wharf – there'd be two, t'ree vessels abreast, waitin' for to get loaded. Then there's a lot o' wharves on the west side o' the LaHave River an' they'd have vessels loadin' all the time. Four masters an' t'ree masters – takin' lumber an' maybe a load o' shingles – takin' 'em to Boston or New York. An' some would be loaded for way down Sout' America, an' to England – some of 'em would be bound for Ireland, takin' lumber an' laths an' pit props for mines, see.

An' then as far as shippin' goes . . . a lot o' places along here used to – they had a dry fish business connected wit' the West Indies. Dry fish an' lumber. The fishermen, most o' the fishermen – that was the salt bankers an' the handliners – a lot o' them vessels, they'd come home from The Banks an' they'd make a trip to the West Indies. Take lumber or salt fish down an' bring salt an' molasses when they come back. Sailed to Barbados, Turks Island, San Juan – all them places. There was boats of all kinds – an' not'in' but sail goin' an' comin' most all the time. Lots o' fellers'd be goin' fishin' on the summer trips – well then fall would come an' they'd go to Lunenburg an' ship on one o' them fishin' vessels goin' sout'. Seen a lot o' hard weat'er there in the Gulf Stream goin' to the West Indies.

We were carryin' lumber an' laths down sout' in the *W.N. Zwicker* – an old t'ree maste[illegible] [illegible]ell, we left here wit' a load o' dry lumber in the hold an' green hemlock on d[illegible] [illegible]e'd generally leave wit' an easterly wind, you know for to sail o'er – but this t[illegible] [illegible]ft in a nor'east wind an' first t'ing that shifted o'er into a sou'east gale o' w[illegible] [illegible] want to tell you, it blew hard. Had to take the sails in – reefed 'em, you see, [illegible] all the sails up an' reefed the fores'l an' the mains'l. Then the wind haule[illegible] [illegible]e to the nor'west an' come a gale from that way. Cold, my good man, it was c[illegible] . . everyt'in' started to freeze up you. An' seas comin' at you every which way.

Well, that spray an' water comin' o'er was freezin' . . . awful cold . . . well, the deck load had about, I'm safe to say, had about a foot of ice all o'er it, y'know. Had to take the mallets to 'er an' pound that ice off. Poundin' an' poundin' like'a that . . . didn't do no good though 'cause water froze onto 'er as fast as we could chop it off. Ice on the deck an' the riggin' . . . everyt'in' was right blue wit' ice. An' the ice made 'er heavy an' she started to wallow in the seas. You know what that means. We was about t'ree hundred miles from home an' it was awful cold . . . an' she filled wit' water. I remember it yet . . . five o'clock in the mornin' on the ninth day o' January she filled. Cap'n said, "Start pumpin' boys" – we had not'in' but hand pumps – "Start pumpin' 'cause she's t'ree parts full o' water now." Those damn ol' pumps wasn't much good, you. She filled right up pretty near full. The anchors an' chains . . . they took the bow down – pulled 'er right down – that she didn't . . . the bow never come out o' the water a'tall. It just wouldn't come up that you could see it . . . bow was all the time down under the water. An' boys, we t'ought we was gone. But the stern kept up . . . the dry lumber in the hold kept her afloat.

Well, the fo'c's'le house, that never come out o' the water a'tall . . . an' the inside o' the cabin house was all awash – it didn't fill right full, see, by the stern keepin' up it didn't fill right full. But the water was washin' back an' fort' into it an' tore everyt'in' out inside. Well, we was on top o' the cabinhouse . . . we had the spanker sail there an' we was tied fast to that most o' the time when it was rough. No place to sleep or not'in'.

That first day . . . when she first filled up y'know we sighted two American vessels – both fishin' vessels, an' one was right handy to where we was driftin'. An' t'other one was o'er on the side of us. Well, it wasn't long before we drifted away from her, but t'other vessel, she was joggin'. But she never paid no attention to us – we had our distress signal up, but she never . . . I don't know if they didn't see it or what . . . they never paid any attention.

Anyways, the Cap'n said, "You t'ink we'd try to sail 'er?"

"Why," I said, "you'd better try somet'in' because we ain't goin' to last long out here." Not'in' to eat – for the first t'ree days we had not'in' but a twelve pound box o' biscuit – an' them didn't last very long between the seven of us.

Well, after a while the weather moderated some . . . an' she'd raise, the stern'd raise in the seas. Water'd come into 'er then would run out. Some o' the fellers an' I managed . . . we got down into the after part – when her stern'd come up, see – an' the first t'ing we got was a barrel o' flour. We got that out on deck an' tied that fast up by the riggin'. An' then we got . . . next we got was a barrel o' potatoes. An' before that, when we seen the cabin was startin' to wash out, we took the cabin stove up on top – was an old Mayflower stove y'know, one o' them round Mayflower stoves. An' we had a little piece o' ham . . . ham was pretty well all gone – just kind o' the rind left of it. Well, we'd go to work an' take flour an' water an' mix that up an' take this ham an' rub it o'er the stove an' bake it on that – that we had to eat the third day.

Anyhow, we were on her five days an' then it got t'ick o' fog. We had no charts. No not'in'. Everyt'in' was washed away, you know. An' . . . started to breeze up then from the south'ard again – 'not'er gale o' wind comin' up. The Cap'n said, "We'll have to try to make land somewhere, go in somewhere." See, a southerly breeze'd bring us in somewheres – push 'er in, you – she couldn't sail like when she was on top o' the water. We went on for a while an' we heard like a breakin' on the shore – the sea washin' on the shore. The Cap'n said, "Well, it's either Cross Island or Indian Island, one o' the two." He judged about where he was. An' he gave me the wheel, an' the rest o' the fellers went as far for'ard as they could for a lookout. "Now," he says to me, "when they sing out, give 'er the full wheel" – she wouldn't tack – you had to jibe 'er around. An' the first t'ing they sung out, "Breakers." An' I give 'er the wheel . . . an' then we started to come out. Well we couldn't come out right the way we went in – the way the wind was. Well, we ended up between Indian Island an' Seal Point – came down inside o' Black Rock, an' there we dropped anchor.

We was onto her five days an' five nights, an' we sailed her back t'ree hundred miles full o' water which is somet'in' I don't t'ink was ever done before. An' I don't believe it's been done since.

I'm goin' to tell you one coastin' trip, you. I'm goin' to tell you this one. I was, oh, twenty-three, twenty-four – I wasn't married then. Wages was low then . . . get a dollar, get a dollar a day. Thirty dollars a month. Charlie Kohler from Lunenburg, he sailed the vessel – the *Antagrel*, that was her name. Went to Bridgewater an' she got loaded wit' lumber . . . but he had no crew. Well he got Elden Bushen in West Dublin – he was mate – an' a German cook, a big man. An' Harris Hardy down here. Was one feller . . . I don't just recall. Let that go – I don't know who he was. An' me, I must o' been crazy or somethin', I guess.

Anyways, they towed 'er down to LaHave up here – anchored 'er up above the Red an' White store in the evenin'. The next day she was goin' to sail. Well, my God, I got aboard – I seen I didn't like . . . I didn't like the Cap'n. I didn't like Kohler . . . funny, he had a kind o' way about him. An' he had this damn dog on deck. An' there was a dory hangin' astern. Harris Hardy . . . if him an' I could o' got a dory off, well . . . we'd'a got our clothes an' we'd'a run away! I'd'a run away! If they put me in jail I'd'a went there! I don't know if they could force you to go back or not. Maybe they could. But we couldn't go aft on account o' this goddam dog. So we had to take the medicine . . . had to make the trip.

Well, next mornin' we got towed out clear o' the land. Goin' to Barbados wit' a load o' lumber. An' boys, what a big load on. An old t'ree master. We got out an' the wind was down here from the sou'west an' we stood off by the wind. No radio, no weather reports – nothin' like that at them times. We got out across the Gulf Stream. Out to the south'ard of Bermuda – well that's about seven hundred miles from here. An' fine! This one night the moon come up an' it was full. I'll never forget it – I can forget some t'ings that I done last week. But that! Goin' along – tops'l an' everyt'ing onto 'er. The moon was big an' round . . . oh, it was beautiful. There was nobody walked around on the moon in them times.

Well, ten o'clock come along an' it started to breeze up somethin' bad. The scud was goin' across the moon just like a streak.

Started at ten o'clock to take in sails. We got the tops'ls in, we got the spanker down, we got the jibs down. Worked some fast you. You could hardly walk o'er the deck – it blowed that hard. After a little while we just had the mains'l up – brand new canvas, you – an' the jumbo. First t'ing the jumbo, it blowed to pieces. In one shake that was gone – sheet parted. What a mess, you! An' t'rough the night this deck load shifted. You see, the big pile o' deck lumber. Didn't go o'erboard . . . it went out o'er the side an' listed off. Four bends of a list. An' the next mornin' it was somethin' for to look at. There was times that you couldn't see . . . you couldn't see a hundred feet. I'm tellin' you the truth. That mornin' I seen this sea hit 'er for'ard . . . an' when that sea struck 'er, I seen the spray go o'er the crosstrees. Anybody would hear me sayin' that I suppose would say, "He's a liar." But I'm not. It was somethin' I'll never forget. There was seas . . . I seen one sea go down across the stern of 'er. If that would o' struck her, God only knows what would o' happened to us. An' we laid there, an' that was on a Saturday – reefed mains'l an' four bends of a list. We had nothin' to eat all day Saturday. See, the cook was cookin' in the fo'c's'le house an' that was awash.

That cook we had, he was all right, a nice man. Lot better'n the Cap'n. But he shoved your food – yes, yes – you got your food . . . there was a square hole about so big an' the cook would shove your food t'rough there. See we slept on the other side o' the fo'c's'le house – an' he shoved your food t'rough that hole. An' there you'd eat, just the same as if you were a pig or somethin' in a pen. Didn't say much about that because I had done it before. The food was all right, that part of it.

Anyways, the pumps was goin' straight on . . . lots o' water comin' in o'er. An' every couple of hours we had to put a life line on an' go down an' set the turnbuckles up on the lower side, where she listed. Couldn't hardly walk o'er the deck . . . half o' the time that riggin' would be right under. What a mess! What a mess!

Sunday mornin' she flopped – the wind flopped out. There was some sea on yet, you. Her layin' o'er on one side, the jumbo blowed to pieces. She was a hard lookin' case. Well, t'rough Sunday then, we started to get sail onto 'er. The wind come around in the east'ard – it got fine. We started for Barbados an' we got there.

An' I liked the place too, it was nice. Got ashore. It was . . . plenty o' girls around there, lots of 'em. I was young, see. An' I was goin' to run away – but I had no money. I hated so to come back in that vessel. I hated to come back. But I seen, I guess, I had no money. Either come back, or stay there an' starve to death. Where would I get fed? I had to go.

Well, we come up to St. Martin's to take on a load o' salt for Lunenburg. I had the wheel steerin' an' this Charlie Kohler come up, you know . . . an' him wit' a big kimono on, he walked back an' fort' past the wheel, just the same as if you were some kind of an animal or somethin'. He wouldn't speak to you, no, no . . . he didn't want . . . a great big kimono on there, a pair o' slippers on . . . he'd go back an' fort' smokin' a cigarette. Me, I had a belt strapped around me with a sheath knife. Would'a been no law, then a lot would o' happened. I hated him so! But he's dead an' gone now – makes a difference. I'm livin' yet.

So, we come up to St. Martin's an' we loaded salt. We was there for a week, you. Had to bring the salt off in boats, small boats. Small bags o' salt . . . two or t'ree buckets in a bag – small white canvas bags. An' that's how we loaded salt! An' then he put us out on a plank, outside . . . to paint this damn old boat. On a plank – t'ree of us – you know, the plank was made like stagin' an' lowered down. An' there we was. Had to paint that old t'ing layin' there, all around . . . put grey onto 'er. We was there a week pretty well.

After the salt was loaded, we left for Lunenburg . . . this old t'ree master. We come along . . . when we was gettin' across the Gulf Stream, oh, it was blowin'. One night her tops'l sheet parted. Tops'l's way up you know. Elden Bushen was on the wheel . . . I was on his watch, in the mornin'. An' he said, "Can you reel that off up there?" Had to get the rope up an' get out on the end . . . way out on the end of the gaff! Didn't know no better! Didn't know no better. If she'd o' give one little slap, the sharks would o' soon had me. I crawled . . . then I could reach it from the outside block. An' I rolled off the tops'l sheet. An' in towards evenin' the fore-tops'l sheet parted. But these ot'er fellers helped me this time. See, the sails should'a been lowered down a little more. We shouldn't o' had to crawl out there! The old sails was fallin' down . . . had a new mains'l on – new canvas – an' that's the only t'ing that was any good. We was gettin' into a heavy nor'easter comin' on. An' all right, we didn't last long. We had to run her back, well back to the sou'east. Quite a ways . . . all night. But then it died out, an' we got back to Lunenburg.

Well, I will never forget it. We come in, goin' to Lunenburg . . . we come along, made along up here to Shelbourne. An' we was comin' down along the shore . . . a ways off land. I didn't care then if she went ashore on any rock that was out there. Well, Elden was all right, but this man I didn't like . . . Kohler was the feller I didn't like. 'Course I didn't want Elden to take me around the neck an' kiss me or anyt'in' like that.

So anyhow, we got in toward Lunenburg an' the moon come up an' the wind was on the west'ard. Beautiful fine night – it was in the winter then. Clear, fine evenin'. We was comin' up Lunenburg Harbour, had all the sails on this old t'ing . . . old t'ree master loaded wit' salt. I t'ought to myself, "I don't care if she runs ashore anywheres. No bother to me as long as I get off." It was in the night, one or two o'clock in the mornin' . . . . There's a lighthouse there – off from that is a shoal, but it's mud. So Kohler, he was up there walkin' back an' fort'. I had the wheel, I done as he told me. He says, "Keep 'er off one point," an' I let 'er come up. But he was there walkin' back an' fort'. Moon was out – a pretty night. Not a cloud up in the sky. First t'ing, we got too far to the wind'ard. Bango! We was ashore. I said, "Good. Here you get ashore an' here you can stay ashore." Well, we got the anchor out an' sent a dory ashore to get a tow boat. In to get the *Mascot* – that was the tow boat – to come get this old t'ing off wit' a load o' salt in 'er. After a while, by George, he got 'er off – pulled down, an' first t'ing, off she went. Well I felt bad that she went off because if it had been rocks an' been blowin', the rocks would o' took the bottom out of 'er . . . she'd soon be off! Not that I had anythin' against the vessel or any o' the rest. But Kohler . . . my God, I didn't like that man.

An' we got in an' we got the t'ing tied up. I got t'irty dollars . . . a month. One dollar a day! That's the money I got. T'irty dollars for a month's pay. Now ain't that somethin'?

I hired a car an' I got home. An' I don't know any more if I had money enough to pay my fare home or not. But I got here.

I was sailin' south that winter wit' Cap'n Hibbert Wamback. It was only six of us – three before the mast an' a mate, a cook an' the skipper. I was only seventeen year old. Had on a load o' herrin' an' dry fish for Gordon Romkey up here – in the winter, why he used to ship 'em out to the West Indies. An' we left here, oh, it was a couple o' days after Christmas. We went to San Juan. An' we had a good trip out. Took a long while them times – all by sail. We was twenty-one days goin' out. We got the fish unloaded an' then from there we went to Turks Island an' brought on a load o' salt an' headed for home.

Well, when we got off the coast here we come into a big storm . . . a hurricane. The vessel wasn't young any more . . . the vessel was gettin' old. When we got in that storm, first t'ing, the fores'l went to pieces. We had anot'er one. So the skipper said, "We'll have to try to get this fores'l off – there's not'in' left of it. An' we'll have to try to get t'other one put on." An' the wind . . . I'll never forget it as long as I live. Anyway we got that one unbent an' we got t'other one bent on. So, after we done that, we hauled the other one back onto what you would call the break o' the vessel. The skipper, he was keepin' a watch out for the big seas. After a while, we was there rollin' this fores'l up – tiein' it up. An' first t'ing the skipper sung out. He says, "Boys look after yourselves! It's a big one!" They all made a rush for to get a'hold o' somethin'. But I didn't make it an' the sea struck me. An' she went all under to the leeward. An' it drove me t'rough under the main boom an' here I was tryin' to get a'hold o' somethin', but I couldn't get a'hold o' nothin'. Why it didn't take me right o'er the leeward rail I don't know. An' I kept grabbin' for to try to get hold o' somethin' in my hands. The skipper was standin' near what they call the fief rail – he had a'hold there. An' after a while I did get a'hold o' somethin' an' boys, I held fast. An' what do you t'ink I had a'hold of? I had a'hold of his foot! I got a'hold of the skipper's foot, an' I held fast. An' that's the only t'ing that saved me.

An' after it was all over, the skipper come to me an' said – he always used to call me Willis . . . my name was Willard but he always used to call me Willis – an' he looked down an' he said, "Willis," he says, "that's the only t'ing that saved you."

I said, "I know it." An' I was all wet . . . never changed no clothes. I still kept on workin'. It didn't frighten me or anythin'. I was pretty plucky an' cheeky then. It was a close call, pretty damn close, you. But we got out o' that mess. An' we got back home here from Turks Island somewheres around the first o' March.

I was goin' down to the West Indies one time in a new vessel loaded wit' pine lumber, dried lumber. An' the vessel right new an' they never put enough ballast into 'er, see. Well, I didn't t'ink much of that, I'm goin' to tell you. We loaded in Shelbourne, an' we went.

An' we caught this awful breeze o' wind. We was on deck where the lumber was, an' one end o' the boards was out o'er the rail . . . had 'er loaded right full – one end was out an' t'other was back. An' I seen the wind, it just snapped them boards right off – caught the ends of 'em an' snapped 'em in two. Them pine boards – wasn't very t'ick, they was t'ree quarter inch boards. The wind just snapped 'em right off.

Well, we was runnin', an' we run t'ree hundred miles off the course. We couldn't leave her come up . . . the seas was got too big, the seas got too high. We wasn't able to come up 'cause she'd tip over, she'd roll over. We had to keep goin'. An' you was more on your back layin' than you was on your feet . . . at the wheel. You had a life line around you an' the sea used to break o'er the stern, an' knock you down. There you laid in the water washin' back an' fort' this way an' that way . . . an' get up on your feet an' get a'hold o' the wheel – keep 'er straight, hold the wheel, keep 'er off, keep 'er straight to the sea. An' you seen 'em comin' behind. You'd say, "That's the last. That's the last one I'm goin' to know about."

Well, you was there half an hour at a time at the wheel. You had to go up for'ard then an' hang onto the riggin'. An' I left the wheel, anot'er feller took it, an' I went up for'ard. We were runnin' on the double reefed fores'l – that's all we had up. An' the Cap'n sung out to me, he said, "Drop the peak halyard. There's a big sea comin' behind." I seen it comin' too. An' he was yellin'.

I said, "You don't know nothin', you son of a bitch." I said to myself, I said, "You don't know nothin'."

I seen the sea comin' an' I knowed if I'd'a dropped the peak that would stop her headway. That would stop her headway – that'd take the wind out'a the sail, spill the wind out . . . the sea would break into 'er so much harder, come right o'er the stern. I said, "No, I'm not goin' to untie the halyard. I'm goin' to leave 'er take it." An' that's a good t'ing I did. She took 'er! An' 'er bow went down under . . . an' she come up just slow. An' we got clear. Oh, what seas, what seas! We run that breeze out . . . t'ree hundred miles off the course. T'ree hundred miles. Run that breeze out an' saved ourselves, you.

Well, this one winter, Cap'n Ruey Sardy called me up an' he said he was makin' a trip south an' he wanted me to go. So we went to Mayagüez – that's on the nor'west side o' the island, Puerto Rico. An' we discharged cargo an' headed back to Turks Island for a load o' salt.

Well t'ree days after we left Turks Island, we run into a lot o' wind . . . an' the vessel sprang a leak. We had to lay the vessel to wit' a double reefed fores'l. Well, the second day we took the hatches off o' the vessel, she was right full o' water – right to the hatches. An' the salt was gone – all melted. We couldn't get nothin' to eat – two stoves was under water. An' we was in danger o' sinkin'. Well, the Cap'n said, "We have to get picked off." All you could do was stay on deck on top o' the water. So it was on the third night – so the third night we seen a ship comin' from the east'ard. I had the watch. An' when I seen this light, I called the old man. Well, he come up an', "Well," he said, "we'll make some flares." What you call flares – take a pole an' take some oil clothes an' tie 'em around the pole. An' then you dip it in oil, light it wit' fire an' take it aloft. We did that. Well, the ship came up inside of us on our starboard side – fine clear night – an' she was about two mile or t'ree mile away from us inside. But she kept goin'. Well, I said to the Cap'n, I said, "She's not goin' to stop."

"No," he said, "it don't seem like."

Well, we had what they call a stays'l – hoists between the two spars of a big boat.

Hundred an' twenty-five yards o' canvas. An' we brought that up out o' the fo'c's'le ... cut it in half an' we put it in what they call the chain locker. The chain locker is what your anchor chain was coiled into. So, we put this canvas on top o' the chain. I went back an' asked the Cap'n how much kerosene we had left. He said, "We got one four-gallon can," an' he said, "we have to be very careful o' that."

I said, "Where is it?" Well, he told me where it was an' I went an' got it. An' one o' the shipmates an' me, we grabbed our sheath knives – he stuck in one side o' the can an' I stuck in t'other. We went around till we met each other – took the top right off o' the can. An' we took the four gallons o' kerosene an' we dumped it right o'er this canvas. We tied some rags onto a gaff handle, lit that an' t'rew it on top o' the oil. It went off. An' the flames went right up around the foremast head ... that would be seventy-five feet high. We had a jumbo up – burnt the jumbo halyards off. An' we had the fores'l up ... burnt the halyards off of that. We was some desperate. Everythin' fell down on deck. The Cap'n said, "Now you done it." I never said a word. Fifteen minutes after that I went on the crosstrees ... took to the riggin' an' went on the crosstrees. An' I looked to where the ship would be. An' I seen a port an' starboard light. I wasn't many seconds before I was down on deck! I told the Cap'n, "She's comin' back."

So it was about forty-five minutes I suppose. The ship was on our port side. An' they spoke from the bridge t'rough a speakin' trumpet. But the language we couldn't understand ... it was a German ship. So he went astern o' the schooner – made a circle an' come back. Second time the feller spoke English. Well the Cap'n talked to 'im – told 'im that we had to get off immediately.

It was two o'clock in the mornin' an' the feller said, "We'll wait till daylight an' pick you off." Well if it would o' come a bad squall, you know, you take in the Gulf Stream, you get them awful bad squalls – rain an' wind with it – if one o' them happened to come along ... the Cap'n, he said, "We have to leave right now. We're awash."

So they went to the wind'ard o' the vessel an' they put out a lifeboat. Nine men come down – big life boat. An' they come aboard, an' looked down into the fo'c's'le. She was right level wit' water an' he says, "We got to get you out o' here as quick as we can." Didn't nobody have to tell us that, you!

So that's what we did – we went aboard the German ship. We was t'ree hundred miles from Turks Island – the handiest land to us would be St. Thomas's. Well, when we was picked up, well from there we went to Veracruz, Mexico. An' from there we come back to Havana. An' from Havana to New York. We were there twelve days in the Sailor's Institution. An' we went to Brooklyn an' came down on a ship that they had runnin' from Halifax to Brooklyn. So, thirty-two days from the time our ship went down – we set 'er on fire before we got off – we got back home. Well, I'll tell you that settled my goin' to sea to the West Indies.

# Submarines Was Near

An' when the war come, a lot o' German submarines come off here . . . blew up, oh, I don't know how many vessels. Wanted the ships' papers, you understand. This one time we was warned in by the patrol boat from Halifax. We was all out in the dories when she came along side the vessel . . . she come as close as he dast to come. She was a big boat . . . an' he had one o' them big long speakin' trumpets. The Cap'n – Murdock Getson was his name – he was told there was an old steam trawler that had guns put onto 'er an' she was steamin' right down off The Banks. An' a submarine besides. It was a fine mornin' too – some o' the men, they heard him out in the dories, but I didn't. I was up ahead o' the bow – the wind blowed away from me. An' Murdock, he didn't pay no attention to it. But our cook, a feller by the name o' Freeman Clattenburg – he's dead now – he heard every word o' that warnin'.

Well, we come aboard off o' the dories . . . as we come aboard, he kept tellin' everybody, "This is your last fishin', boys, today. I'm goin' to cook," he said, "as long as we're here to get underway an' go home. But then I'm t'rough. I ain't goin' to cook for no fishin'." Well, he kept tellin' everybody that. An' there was a couple that didn't t'ink anyt'ing of it a'tall. An' the second hand – Will Huey back here from Mount Pleasant – he was anot'er one to join the skipper . . . he didn't t'ink there was anyt'ing to it. But we knowed about the war, you see, an' we knowed we should head for in.

Anyway, dinnertime come an' Murdock, he never come in the companionway to say a word – "Are you goin' out?" or "You want to go home?" or anyt'ing a'tall. An' Will Huey, he come down an' says, "You ain't goin' out fishin' no more?"

Well, we told him, "No." See, it was no good to fish – we was out there about two hundred miles. It was quite a sail, that time o' year, you know . . . sometimes you don't get much wind for t'ree or four days. An' we didn't know where the submarine was . . . .

We had our minds made up. We figured, "There ain't no use listenin' to them.

We got to get the hell out o' this." That's just what we did. An' we wasn't long puttin' the sails on, I'll tell you! An' boys, t'ings was a'flyin'. Yes sir. An' Murdock stood back . . . he never said a word. I'll never forget that. All the principle fellers was back in the cabin . . . that's where they all slept, you understand . . . in the cabin. Well there was seven or eight of us down in front an' we all said, "If they don't want to come for'ard, the hell with 'em – we'll find Nova Scotia. We won't miss the whole place." An' we finally did make land. Made Canso.

We had about t'ree days fishin' yet, for that, an' then we'd have our full trip. An' this mornin' – the twentieth day of August it was – we went out in our dories. We went out in our dories an' Eli Oxner an' I, the two of us, went off in one direction, you understand, an' all the rest o' the dories was up, way up from us. An' we went 'bout a mile from the vessel till we anchored . . . an' Eli said to me, he said, "What is that there comin'?"

"Why," I said, "that looks like a fish dragger, a fish dragger there comin'." An' she kept comin' towards us. I soon found out it wasn't no fish dragger. Well, these two American vessels laid near by our vessel, an' the one Cap'n must'a known, must'a mistrusted somethin'. He put more sails on his vessel an' started in for land. An' all at once it just . . . just . . . the boat that had the gun on its bow, fired at the vessel. An' a cannonball went just ahead o' the vessel . . . drove the water up. An' you, he didn't notice nothin' – he kept right on. An' the next time this boat fired, it took the whole fo'c's'le right out o' that vessel . . . an' then he got . . . he had to give up then. Brought the vessel up an' hove to. Well this boat that had the gun on the bow – there was two of 'em, a submarine was along side – she went there an' sank that vessel. An' sank the other American vessel. Put the men off in their dories an' sank the two vessels.

Well, the submarine came up on the side of our vessel. Oh, she was a big concern, a big concern, you. Our men that was in the dories, when they seen what was goin' on, they pulled off. They wouldn't come down nowheres nigh for to see on account of they t'ought they might lose their life or somet'in' t'rough it. So they kept on goin' right in for land. An' I said to Eli, I said, "They didn't hurt the Americans an' they won't hurt us. Let's go up to see what they're doin'." An' we rowed up to our vessel . . . I would say about ten yards we stopped from her, you, an' watched everythin' that was doin'. The submarine laid right out there, out o' the water – stuck right out o' the water, you. An' they took all our clothes – we used to have trunks, you know, wit' our good clothes in – they took an' carried 'em back an' put 'em in a dory. Well then they hauled the flag down an' they rolled it up an' t'rowed that down in the dory – all that kind o' stuff, they took it o'er an' put it aboard the submarine.

Then they come back, an' they took the bomb, an' they put the bomb down o'er the stern o' the vessel. But they had a line to it – they brought the line up, around, an' tied it to the main riggin'. An' they jumped in the dory an' rowed across an' went aboard the submarine an' sent the dory adrift. An' all at once we felt just . . . just a shiver. The bomb must'a went off, you understand. An' our vessel went down stern first. The stern went right under . . . under . . . she kept goin' under, under. Last t'ing we saw was the bowsprit. Eli an' me, we started for in. We put the sail on the dory an' headed for land – we had a long ways to go.

An' we sailed all the rest o' that afternoon, we sailed all that night, an' the next mornin'. I stood up an' looked for . . . see if I could see anythin'. Couldn't see nothin'. No boats, none of our dories . . . nobody on salt water. So we kept on goin'. An', oh, about two o'clock in the afternoon I stood up on the t'wart again an' looked. I said, "Eli, I see a vessel comin' towards us. Fair for us. Out from land." An' we kept on goin'. She was comin' out an' we was goin' in . . . right fair for her. An' when we got close to him, he let his vessel come up – the head to the wind an' made signs for to come aboard. An' when we went up aboard o' the vessel, he said, "Boys," he said, "what happened?" We told him, you know . . . a submarine sank our vessel. An' that it was sinkin' all the vessels that's off there. Well, he jumped right clear o' the deck. He said, "Get the vessel around! Put all the sail onto 'er you can put!" There was hollerin' you! We started the vessel in for land. An' they took us down for'ard then – gave us all they could give us to eat. An' they took us in – we got in – that night after dark – we got into Canso. But the rest of our crew an' the ot'er two crews off of the American vessels never got in till the next mornin'. See they had to row an' sail all o' the distance, you, from The Banks in. So we stayed there all night aboard that vessel – we had no place to go. An' the next mornin', the next mornin', we took the ferry boat an' went up to Mulgrave, an' there we took the train an' we came t'rough to Halifax. An' when they found out what happened to us, everybody tried to use us good.

Well, when we got to Halifax, there is places in there – Sailors' Rest it's called an' this an' that. But, you see, there was so many fishermen comin' in, they had everythin' filled up. We was walkin' the sidewalk . . . we had no place to go into. This policeman come along an' he said, "Boys," he said, "I'd like to do somethin' for you," he said, "an' I can if you want to go wit' me."

We said, "All right, we'll go wit' you." An' we went up to the police station.

"Now," he said, "that's the best I can do for you. There's the cells if you want'a lay down to have a rest."

"Fine."

An' we set there talkin' t'ings o'er, an' by an' by, there was a rap come to the door an' a man come in an' he said, "You're the men that's submarined?"

We said, "Yes."

An' he went out again – he was only gone a couple o' minutes. He come back an' he had two bottles o' drink – rum, you, the finest kind – an' the glasses an' two packs o' cards, an' he said, "Now have a good time." An' we did have a good time from that to daylight.

Well, the next . . . after daylight then, he took us to the train an' we come up near Bridgewater. There was a man by the name o' Joseph Bush out home, an' my brother Spenser, an' myself – we was the t'ree that come out there. Creation! On the trains comin' along – when the people got word about it, you – they come 'round us, an' there was some askin' for to get the story. When we got to Bridgewater, we was home, I call it. I knew people there in Bridgewater, the restaurants an' this an' that – went down, we told the feller there what happened, an' we had no money, an' he said, "Haul in." In the name o' creation, he started to carry the food to us. It was somethin' to look at, you. An' we wasn't shaved for weeks, you, an' I said to Joseph Bush there, "Now we'll go for a haircut an' a clean up." Went o'er to the barber shop, an' I told the barber what was up, an' he said, "Set down. The t'ree o' you, set down." We set down an' they cut our hairs an' shaved us an' they prettied us all up. So now I said to Joseph Bush, I said, "We have to get some way to get home." We had a long ways from Bridgewater out to the islands.

Well we met a man by the name o' Harry Mosher from the lighthouse out there. "Oh," he said, "I'll take you down to your home."

T'ought, "Fine."

Got in aboard the motor boat an' we come down the river, an' the farther we got down the river, the harder it blew. "Well," I said, I said to Harry, "there's a gale o' wind outside that point. I'm sure we won't get up o'er the bay." That's Dublin Bay. An' when we got down to LaHave, we saw anot'er boat there from the islands – man by the name o' Louis Walfield. "Well," Harry said, "I'll tell you what I'll do." He said, "That'll be a long ways for me to go – o'er to the island. Why not take you in an' put you aboard o' that boat?"

"Fine." Louis had to go right on home there to the islands. "That'd be fine."

When we got aboard this ot'er boat an' we come around Fort Point, it was a livin' hurricane. Sou'west. The water, the spray was a'flyin'. We got half ways up o'er the bay when the engine broke. An' I said to Joe, Joe Bush, I said, "If I ever get . . . . "

The man that owned the boat there, he said, "We got to go back to LaHave. We can't do it, there's no way o' gettin' home." He said, "I got to take the boat to LaHave an' get the engine repaired."

An' I said to Joe, "If I ever get my feet on dry land, no one'll ever get no salt water on me no more."

Anyway we got back in LaHave, an' when the boat was tied to the wharf, the t'ree of us jumped out an' we started to walk. An' we walked up to what they call Bell's Cove down here an' there we got a dory. From there we rowed out to the islands, an' went home. An' all the people felt some bad. They got the news, you understand, an' they didn't know if we was goin' to get to land in an arrangement like that – all the vessels gettin' sunk. It wouldn't'a been half bad if we had somethin' for to get the news – like nowadays, why, you'll hear everythin' that's goin' on. But nobody knowed nothin', nothin' a'tall . . . them days we didn't hear about how the war was goin' or anythin'.

Anyway, I did get home.

DECEMBER

Belanger
EUREKA

RITCEY BROTHERS LIMITED
NOVEMBER
RITCEY & CREASER

IN MEMORY
OF
SAMUEL J.
SON OF
RACHEL
AND THE LATE
JOSEPH HECKMAN
LOST AT SEA
OCT. 1883.
AGED 25 YRS.
The sea shall give up
its dead

We was on St. Pierre Bank. I was wit' Fred Richard in *The Gloaming* – his t'ird year master. We only had one day fishin' more. I t'ink we had about . . . fifty quintals would'a made a trip. Had enough salt for that. Was on a Sunday evenin'. The patrol boat come up – ordered us off o' The Bank. Said the submarines was near, an' we should get off o' The Bank. Well, there was a lot o' the crew members said, "Well, how are the German submarines goin' to get way over here?" So they didn't pay any attention. An' that was Sunday evenin'.

Well, when Monday mornin' come, we got our breakfast four o'clock to get ready to go in the dories. But some of us come to the table there all dressed up in their good clothes – which I was one o' them. So the Cap'n come down an' he said, "I guess you men is all t'rough fishin' by the way it looks."

"Yes. We was ordered off The Bank an' why not take the order?"

Well, this was four o'clock in the mornin' . . . little breeze sou'west. An' he got mad y'know. He stayed there till nine o'clock in the mornin' – waitin' to see if we'd put the dories o'er. Well then he said we'd get the anchor. So we got the anchor – an' we was about two hours till we got the dories shifted ahead on the main deck an' we got the sails hoisted for home.

An' it was around eleven o'clock, dinnertime – I was for'ard takin' the leads off my lines, an' the Cap'n, he was just comin' o'er the deck. The fog was t'ick . . . it gave a gleam, you know, like you see it sometimes in the west'ard. An' I just happened to look that way, I guess. An' here was this t'ing on the water. Well I said to the Cap'n, I said, "What's that up there, an old barge?" He never spoke, you. He turned as white as a ghost. He turned an' went down into the cabin an' he brought the flag up an' he t'rowed it across the main boom. Well, about that time then, the submarine was down to the vessel . . . she had seen us. They went across the bow an' they said, "Ten minutes. All hands leave the ship." An' them men the night before said the submarines couldn't get o'er here, well them was the men that didn't have any courage at that time. Now they were just doomed.

The submarine came along side an' he told the Cap'n to come aboard the submarine – bring a dory an' come aboard. So, which he did – the old man, he left. He told us, he said, "You fellers t'row out all the dories you can 'cause we'll need 'em for goin' in." So we t'rowed out what we could get out . . . till they come back. I went down for'ard an' got a box. The cook had a lot o' food baked up . . . I just took my arms an' scooped the food right into the box. I gave it to a feller on deck an' I said, "Put that in our dory." An' they had a coffee pot – twenty-six men – would hold about four gallons . . . well I wrenched that out an' I filled it wit' fresh water. So I took that up the steps an' I said, "Put that in the dory." Which he did. Well about that time then the Cap'n was back along side wit' t'ree officers . . . they had belts on an' pistols hangin' in the belts. They come up on deck an' took the hatches off an' seen that the vessel was full o' fish an' they made a hearty laugh an' that was it. I walked back aft to where the compass was . . . where the Cap'ns most generally laid their spy glasses an' I said to myself, "Well, I'll take that – might do me some good before we get someplace." So I put the spy glasses in my pocket, an' was walkin' to where the dory was an' one o' these Germans come along an' took the spy glasses out o' my pocket. He took it! An' they took the navigation gear – the chronometer, the sextant, an' that stuff that belonged to the Cap'n.

Anyway, one o' the officers, he passed . . . the bomb up . . . that they put under the vessel. It had a face onto it, the same as a clock, an' some more knobs . . . I suppose for to set it. An' they took a line an' they lowered it down under the stern. An' they tied the line fast to the main riggin'. The crew was all off but t'ree of us an' the Cap'n – we was still aboard the vessel when this happened. The Cap'n said to one o' the officers, he said, "I got no cap. Could I go down an' get a cap?"

He said, "Go down an' get all your clothes if you t'ink you got time." Well, they was Germans but they talked just as good English as what I'm talkin'.

So the Cap'n went down an' got a cap an' he got some o' his clothes. An' we left. We stayed, oh, about two miles away . . . from the vessel. There was no explosion that we could hear . . . but we felt it. Almost lifted the dory out o' the water. Now we was ninety, ninety-five miles from land. We was on St. Pierre Bank, an' the handiest land – Langley Island – was nine mile west o' St. Pierre. Every dory had a compass, but the Cap'n he said, "I'll steer the course," an' you know, the dories would follow him. Around twelve o'clock it breezed up – a lot o' wind. We had to heave to an' cut our sails down . . . take about five feet off o' the spar an' about t'ree, four feet off o' the boom. Tie 'em in, see. At six o'clock we heard the horn on this island an' about nine o'clock we got ashore.

There was a bank – suppose it'd be close to a hundred feet – we had to get up o'er. Hauled the dories up. An' we climbed the bank. An' it was one old gentleman that we come across. An' when he seen us comin' o'er the bank . . . well he made an alarm. So when we got to the houses, there wasn't a soul to be seen. They had all fled, you. See they t'ought we was Germans. On the back end o' the island about a mile back from where the lighthouse an' the firehouse was, was a woods. That's where they went. Well, by an' by one o' the crew members got handy enough to one o' these fellers . . . an' he told him what happened.

Well, then meal time come . . . each family took as many as they could feed. An' when nighttime come, why we wondered where we was goin' to sleep. But there was one old feller an' he said, "Come wit' me."

An' he took us out in the barn. They had some small horses there – I believe they come from Sable Island. An' they had goats, they had hens, they had pigs. Well, we went up into a loft . . . there was twenty-four of us in the crew. An' the barn was full o' hay upstairs. Well, we were there four days . . . we slept in the barn, four nights. But you're very glad to be in a place like that after what happened, you know. From there we got to St. Pierre an' from there, home.

But it wasn't so nice. You know, to lose all your clothes an' all that fish an' everythin' gone to the bottom. Nothin' to live on, you. Nothin'. An' that's how it went . . . fishin' durin' the war.

# I Had to Laugh

We went off the vessel, five or six of us. An' we kind o' went in company – just huntin' for fish you know. An' we had an old feller aboard by the name o' John Hemian from Sandy Point. He didn't have no compass – he didn't know the compass. But you couldn't fool him.

Well, we started back for the vessel. An' by an' by we got up to him – he talked kind o' short you know. "Where you goin'? Where you goin'?" He said, "Where you goin'?"

"Why, we're goin' aboard."

"Keep on goin' that way," he said. "You'll get aboard! You'll strike 'er!"

Well, in a little piece, we looked at where we were goin' . . . we was wrong. The old feller knowed it all along – so we turned 'round an' rowed after him an' he was goin' to the vessel an' we was goin' the ot'er way away from him. I had to laugh at him.

I can remember him sayin' that yet.

What we went t'rough . . . what we went t'rough for what we got was enough to kill you. Wet, you – we was wet an' stiff. An' you go in the bunk an' sleep – you'd be sleepin' a while – an' the first t'ing. Just good in the bunk sleepin'. An', "Squid ho!" Squid. Bait. I'll never forget one night I run up on deck. We got a few squid all right. An' I had a piece o' loaf cake in my mouth – in my hand, an' I went to put it in my mouth. An' the first t'ing the feller next to me jigged up a squid, an' why the damn t'ing squirted juice right on it. Right on the cake, you. Oh my! Oh my!

At handlinin' on The Banks when you went there you was there till you come home. An' many's the time – especially when you was fishin' down off o' Newfoundland – you'd never see the sun. For weeks, nothin' but fog, fog, fog. An' for them skippers, when you was ready to come in – when you made your trip – it didn't make any difference if it was t'ick or t'in. You headed for land. An' listen, when you was ready for back, you always made it. It's a hard t'ing to do. You'd be out there a couple o' months shiftin' from one place to anot'er tryin' to find some fish. An' very seldom did a vessel go astray.

Them old Cap'ns had nothin' for to navigate wit'. Nothin' but a compass an' a deep sea lead. That's all – and an outfit for to take the sun. When they t'ought they was in shallow water, they'd t'row their deep sea lead o'erboard an' they had marks on the line – twenty fat'om, thirty fat'om, forty fat'om. Every ten fat'om they had a mark – tell you how deep the water was.

An' I'll tell you somethin' else. The old skippers, they used to throw a chip o' wood o'erboard an' walk aft. You see if they got astern before the chip, they'd know they was goin' faster than four miles an hour. That way they'd tell how fast they was goin'.

That's the way they done it. An' like I said, not very often they didn't make where they run for. And today! The equipment they got . . . . Well, they say about the older people, they didn't have education an' . . . . But somebody must o' had it. These people that are in charge o' the draggers . . . if they go out an' their gear breaks down, why it seems they got some trouble to get in, some o' them. Today, they'll be in the school house until they're twenty-three, twenty-four years old . . . in the navigation school. Well now, wait till I tell you. There was a dragger over here in Riverport this summer. The Cap'n stayed ashore an' gave the boat in charge o' this feller that had all this learnin'. He knowed everythin'. This an' that – everythin'. Went to school all that length o' years. He got down aboard the dragger an' he told the crew to untie 'er. He turned around in Riverport an' instead o' goin' out 'round Fort Point out to sea, he kept goin' up the river. When the crowd commenced to look, they was goin' inland on the river, an' they commenced to talk. "Where are we goin' to? We have to do somethin' – say somethin'." They asked him where he's goin'.

"Where are we goin'? Why we're goin' out on The Banks!"

They said, "No, you're goin' to Bridgewater." Steamin' right up the river. He turned around, you.

I was in only one dory that ever filled. And that's the only one that ever I was in any danger all the time I went fishin'. Me an' my dory mate, we was trawlin' on The Banks an' the wind blowin' here from the sou'east. An' snowin'. Dirty weat'er an' heavy seas runnin'. Haulin' an' baitin', haulin' an' baitin'. And all the time the wind gettin' worse. Well, we was about to head for in – had a good load o' fish – when this sea struck o'er us. Piled right in o'er the bow an' filled 'er, you. She set low, see, 'count o' the fish into 'er.

"Grab a bucket!" I said, "Bail."

"We can't bail 'er. We're lost."

"We can bail 'er," I said, "take the tub an' when she rolls, roll the water out." She was awash see. Water comin' in an' goin' out. When a dory's under water like that she's not'in' but water. We was standin' in the water. It was a damn good chance that we couldn't save 'er, that she would go down.

"We're lost. We're lost," he said.

"We ain't lost if we bail," I said. "Keep bailin'." Some o' the fish was goin' at the same time, out I guess wit' the buckets. By an' by she got up out o' the water a little so's the water kept from comin' in.

"We've got 'er now," I said. "Get what fish is left o'erboard an' start buckin' for the vessel." We started rowin'. An' it wasn't a bit o' sea then. It was right smooth . . . all full o' froth on the water where it had broke . . . leveled everyt'ing off.

Well, we got aboard. The two of us right soaked you know.

The old man come down . . . he come down an' said, "Go below boys an' get some tea." Listen you, we got down an' my dory mate looked at me an' says, "My soul, my teeth's gone." Had false teeth, you know. He was so frightened he didn't know he lost 'em. "Yes," he said, "my soul, I lost 'em."

I said, "They were lost out o' your mouth when that sea struck. You was so scared they jumped out o' your mouth an' you didn't even see 'em go."

"Yes," he said, "by heavens, you're right."

Lost his teeth, you, an' didn't know it!

Cap'n John Parker – he wanted a cook. An' down on the wharf there he seen a policeman he was well-acquainted wit'. This feller said he'd give 'im a cook. The skipper said all right. An' the policeman got 'im a cook. Right the next day he sailed.

Well, he got outside – this feller never cooked in 'is life – knowed not'in' about cookin'. Cap'n John Parker, he said, "The Lord sent the food, but the Devil sent the cooks." Summer trip, you – t'ree months – an' this man couldn't cook. No.

The Cap'n wanted a crew cook an' so he learned this feller, learned 'im to make ship victualin'. He got along good enough to make ship victualin'.

An' when he got back, Cap'n Parker got a'hold o' this policeman an' he said to this feller, he said, "Where did you get this cook from?"

To top it off, why he said, "Why he's my own brother. Walkin' around wit' no job. Had no work. I told 'im there was a good job – you go to cook aboard that vessel."

There was a vessel out o' the river. An' they had bad characters – well, they was wild fellers – some o' them young fellers from the river, they were pretty wild, for tricks, you know, playin' tricks, full o' devilment, you. An' they wanted to stay into land, see. Courtin' y'see they was. Wanted to stay the next couple o' nights wit' the girls.

Well, the vessel was in want of a cook, so the Cap'n went ashore, an' he got a feller down. He said, "We better lay in tomorrow to try 'im, see if he can do anyt'ing." An' he was a half-decent cook. Well, these young fellers, they watched to see what he was makin'. This one mornin' he made clam chowder. The chowder was done, an' he set it back on the stove, see, an' went up on deck an' he'd ring the bell for the crowd to get out. An' while he went on deck, the one feller came off the bunk an' put a whole package o' pepper in the soup. Well, the cook, he never looked in, an' served it off – he dipped this soup up in a big dish an' put it on the table. They all gathered 'round the table. The Cap'n he come down. Almost killed 'im! Well the Cap'n said, "Cook," he said, "there's a lot o' pepper in this."

"I don't t'ink there's a lot o' pepper into it," he said.

The Cap'n, he said, "Taste it." Couldn't eat a bit of it. They chased him off, you. Chased him off.

An' well, they had to hunt around for anot'er feller. An' these young fellers from the LaHave River, they said, "If anot'er cook comes, we're goin' to serve him just the same." Well they got anot'er feller. An' he made a crock o' beans. They watched him an' when they seen their chance they put a pile o' salt in – awful lot o' salt put in. An' when the beans was done, they set down for supper. He set the crock right on the table – earthen crock y'know. Holds two gallons. An' he came to dip up the beans – oh, the salt! They chased 'im off! Chased two cooks off before they'd let one be. Just for the girls, you!

Frank an' I was dory mates for t'ree years. You know he's a feller you could tell him about mostly anyt'ing an' he would take it for granted, you know. An' one day we was sailin' down here to the wind'ard an' we was sailin' down pretty easy. An' Frank was steerin' the dory. An' I was settin'. We had a middle load o' fish. So this day – I always, you know, had somethin' to say to make times go fast. Always somethin' foolish or anot'er. So we were haulin' along an' I said, "Frank, I'll tell you what we'll do. Let's sell our women."

Frank said, "No, I won't sell my wife!"

I said, "Why not? Fifty or a hundred dollars is a lot o' money."

"What the hell would I do wit' my children?" See they was all little then.

"Well," I said, "somebody would look after them."
I'll say there was no way. He t'ought a lot of his wife. There was no way he'd sell his wife!
So, oh . . . about the week after that one day we was out. We got in a hard spot an' it was all . . . it was hard, goin' hard. An' Frank was in the bow an' I could see, boys, he was . . . he was pullin' every inch that was into 'im – he was a small man, mind you – to get this goddam trawl hauled. A lot o' fish. So I t'ought, "Now's the time again." I said, "Frank, would you sell your wife?"
"Jesus Christ," he says, "I'd give her away!"

Well, my old dad, he'd come o'er here wit' us sometimes. An' he would tell stories of t'ings that happened – was supposed to of happened. Ghosts an' one t'ing an' anot'er. An', Mary would look at him. "Now, Grampa," she'd say, "you don't believe that, do you?" An', you know, he would get half mad. Yes sir, he'd get half mad.
He was sayin' one time there was a place – an apple tree in a graveyard. An' it was always loaded wit' sweet apples . . . an' nobody could ever get any apples off o' this tree. So he got a feller by the name of Sollie Winter – he's dead an' gone. An' they run to shore off o' this vessel they was on to get these apples . . . went ashore to see what was happenin'. So the old dad, he was right full o' the Old Nick, you know. An' the old dad says, "Sollie, you go up an' shake the tree. An' I'll pick up what falls." An' when Sollie got up on top o' the tree an' started shakin', the old man he started to run. Said, "Sollie, come on, there's somethin' after us!" An' Sollie didn't wait to climb down the tree. He jumped. An' when he jumped he struck his feet on an old grave an' it broke an' down he went into the ground – oh, t'ree or four feet! An' I guess that he was near – he near had the kannipshuns!

The men used to spend the week in a little shack out here on Cape LaHave. Be closer to where they fished, see. Wouldn't have to row so far. Shore fishin', they was. Well, I'd go out Sunday evenin's wit' 'em – I was only fourteen – for the week you know. Take a bag o' bread out wit' molasses – 'bout all we had was bread an' molasses . . . wit' some sugar, butter we'd take too.
The old men believed into ghosts an' them t'ings – they used to hear t'ings out there – McCleods Harbour. An' they'd sit around in the evenin' talkin' 'bout ghosts an' the Devil.
So anyway, why I used to have to get breakfast – out there in the mornin', you see. Go to the well for a bucket o' water. An' right down o'er the bank was a . . .

they said was a man buried there. An' I was always scared to go back to this well when it was dark – expectin' to see this man. So anyway, this mornin', I went back for a bucket o' water for to get breakfast. An' it wasn't quite daylight yet. I had to go up o'er a little hill an' there was gooseberry bushes was as high as I was there. An' just as I ris' up o'er the hill, there was somethin' grabbed me by the shoulders here! I t'ought the Devil had me for sure! Well I didn't faint . . . well almost. An' I felt somet'in' warm, you see. "Well," I t'ought, "it can't be a ghost." Well! It was that big dog we had out there! His face was along side o' mine lickin' my cheek. A big brown dog we had there. It was so tickled to death to see me – put his two paws up on top o' my shoulders. But that was an awful sensation you know! That was quite a sensation, you. That was the time the ghost grabbed me.

# The August Breeze

We went to bed that evenin' – evenin' of the seventh of August 1926 – an' around here there wasn't one t'ing to be seen when we went to bed. Ca'm an' stars was out, you – there wasn't no signs of any storm or anyt'ing. An' when we got up in the mornin' why, we looked o'er into the cove o'er here, an' there – there was Ed Walfield's boat gone ashore. An' all t'rough that day the wind kept gettin' worse an' there was a big swell on . . . it was an awful storm that day an' that night it was worse. Yes sir, we had t'ings bad here but out on The Banks . . . well, I guess you couldn't know how terrible it was unless you was there. Anyways, the next day, the eighth it was . . . we didn't know anyt'ing first in the mornin' . . . but as the day went on, why we heard of all the men bein' lost off o' Sable Island. See, the storm come up so quick . . . nobody had no warnin' . . . not even a radio . . . why, if the men knowed somet'in' like that was comin' why they could of . . . they could of got off The Banks somewhere an' got out o' that shoal water. An' it would o' been altoget'er different. Probably the biggest part of it wouldn't of happened.

My God . . . all them vessels caught in that hurricane o' wind . . . what didn't go ashore on Sable Island I guess swamped at anchor. There was six vessels that went down . . . they claim it was in the reach of one hundred men that drowned in that gale. From here . . . two vessels . . . the *Sylvia Mosher* an' the *Sadie Knickle* wit' all hands . . . Cap'n John Mosher on the *Sylvia Mosher* an' Cap'n Charlie Corkum – he was skipper on the *Sadie Knickle*. Right from around here was quite a few men that got gone. Here I guess it was about the worst it was anywhere . . . was about the most, y'know for one little place . . . it was quite a few from here on them vessels.

1926 the August Gale was. I had been fishin' wit' Cap'n John Mosher on the *Sylvia Mosher*. An' when we had the fish taken out in Lunenburg on the last trip I made wit' him, Cap'n John called us all down there in the cabin. He said, "Now come back men," he said, "in the cabin. I want to see who's goin' wit' me next summer." We all went back an' when it come my turn, he asked me, "Ernest," he says, "will you make the trip wit' me?"

"No," I said, "Cap'n, no I'm not goin' wit' you."

"Well," he said, "why don't you go wit' me?"

"Well," I said, "it's nothin' a'tall. I'm not goin' handlinin'."

"I'd like for you to go wit' me." He coaxed me hard that afternoon for me to go wit' him.

"No," I said.

"Is it anythin' on my part?"

I said, "There's nothin' on your part. You're the nicest man that I ever went wit'. I'm just takin' a change."

So I went trawlin' wit' a man down from Riverport there, Cap'n Mossman. If I'd'a said yes to Cap'n John Mosher, I wouldn't be settin' here now. In the winter my two brothers, my youngest brother, Guy an' my oldest brother Caleb shipped on the *Sylvia Mosher* an' they stayed wit' her. An' on the seventh of August – when that August Gale was – they was at Sable Island. An' the vessel got caught in that August Gale there . . . never heard tell of it no more. They say the *Sylvia Mosher* was ready for to leave down off o' Sable Island. She was loaded wit' fish an' ready for to leave to come home, you see. But they didn't get left. The storm come up that night . . . an' it come up so quick that it took 'em. That's a hard spot, you . . . the winds was o'er a hundred miles an hour. Maybe if they got out in deeper water somewheres they might o' stood a better show . . . but they couldn't get out o' that. My brothers . . . all hands . . . then the *Sadie Knickle* was lost in the same gale. They was lost, all hands . . . there was nothin'.

I was out in that August Breeze when all the men got lost, when the *Sylvia Mosher* got lost. I had two brothers and an uncle onto 'er when she broke up. We was only five miles from them . . . that was all . . . five miles. An' they got lost an' we got back. That was a bad one, I'm tellin' you. The words can't tell how bad it was.

The Cap'n, he gave up . . . t'ought there was nothin' to be done to save us. He done good, he was doin' brave . . . but he just couldn't . . . . An' Moyle Randall, he took over. Had to cut the cable. See, she was pullin' herself to pieces goin' into the seas . . . seas poundin' right o'er her. She was leakin' bad. We knowed if she'd hung to the anchor, she would'a sunk, she would'a sunk. An' he watched his chance an' he cut the cable. An' she went backwards a little, put 'er stern under an' 'er bow fell off. An', he told us to hoist the jumbo, an' we was runnin' right off the wind, right straight off the wind. An' she made nine knot an hour goin' off the wind under the bare poles – nothin' but the jumbo on.

An' . . . we had a lot o' young fellers on an' they got frightened, you know. They wouldn't come on deck. I'd say about half o' the crew . . . we worked for our lives. I'm goin' to tell you. You either had two t'ings to do . . . work for your life, or go down.

There was nothin' battened down, you understand . . . nothin' tied down. We wasn't lookin' for this storm. Wasn't lookin' for it . . . had no warnin', you see. An' we had twenty-one dories – we had four nests o' dories – twenty-one dories on the cabin house on both sides, lashed to the main boom. An' one sea come . . . an' that sea took the twenty-one dories, the main boom, everythin' went o'er the side. That one sea. Broke right acrost 'er. Raised up the cabin house where we could crawl right down in the cabin off the deck. I would say about eight men were on deck when that sea come . . . but we seen 'er comin'. Every man went up the riggin' to save ourselves . . . all we could do . . . we t'ought that was the last of us. But she come out of it.

Then we had to keep her off more – all that water pourin' in. An' we got hammers an' boards to nail that hole up where the sea had broke the cabin house out. Was nothin' on deck . . . everyt'in' was cleaned right off. An' then the next sea come after we were runnin' a while . . . an' that took the fore hatch. An' anot'er come an' took the booby hatch an' the two hatches right out o'er the rail. An' here the hatch was wide open. An' the sea was comin' down in that fore hatch an' washin' t'rough the hold . . . smashed everyt'in', you. The fish – an' this is true, mind you – some o' the fish was washed up in the top bunk in the fo'c's'le. An' we got hammers an' boards . . . we covered that hatch up. Oh, we was gettin' jogged around you.

I'll tell you, sometimes it looked bleak. Well, I had a suit o' Black Diamond oil clothes. An' that was a Saturday afternoon that we cut the cable. On Sunday mornin', the only t'ing left was just the collar around my neck. That's true as I set here. Oil clothes was tore off me. Right in there o'er the nor'west bar of Sable Island we went. See, we were shovin' clear o' the nor'west bar but we had to keep her off so she wouldn't fill . . . we went o'er shoal water. I never seen nothin' like it. Somehow we got clear of it . . . my brothers an' uncle, they wasn't so lucky. Most everyone around here had family lost in that gale . . . family an' friends gone so quick.

We was fishin' that day out there to the south'ard o' Sable Island in twenty-nine fathom o' water. That was wit' Cap'n Murdock Getson on the *Silver Thread.* An' there was seas I'm safe to say a hundred feet high. An' in the afternoon when we was out in our dories we was up to the wind'ard o' the vessel. An' when she would go down in a swell, you could just see her topmast truck . . . the main top truck. Well, the mainmast is ninety feet an' that was up thirty feet more. That shows how much swell it was. That was the August Breeze when all them vessels was lost.

Anyway, we got aboard an' we got our fish dressed down – nine o'clock. That evenin' we had a hundred an' eighty-five fat'om o' cable out . . . that much scope. We was layin' to, at anchor. An' boys there was some water comin' in o'er the decks. An' at eleven o'clock the cable parted about three fat'om from the anchor. An' that made 'er get side to it. First t'ing, she made three rolls – three slaps. The wind caught the storms'l an' it was gone . . . not'in' but the selvedges left. That's all. Took it out like a bang!

And . . . all the crew was below. I went on watch . . . nobody would go on deck. I took that job. Nobody wouldn't take it an' I said, "Where's my oil clothes? Somebody's got to take it." I got out, an' first t'ing I was o'erboard an' my oil clothes filled wit' water – had my oil pants tied down around my boots an' when I got o'erboard, you see, them blowed out an' filled full o' water. Well, she rolled o'er an' I got a'hold o' the lanyards an' got back aboard. I was lucky . . . more'n lucky. I didn't lose my head – I grabbed a rope an' I fastened it 'round my waist. An' I fastened that to the main boom . . . if the main boom would o' went, why I guess I'd'a went wit' it. An' I stood watch there from eleven o'clock in the night till five the next mornin'. An' there wasn't a man come to relieve me. They said they couldn't come on deck . . . even if she was goin' down. They'd o' gone down wit' 'er.

Well, I poured oil on the deck an' that run off t'rough the scuppers – made a ca'm slick. The sea wouldn't break. Oil smoothens it, see . . . that it comes a'roll all right, but it don't come no sharp rolls an' cut – don't roll up an' smash down. An' that's the way you ca'med it down.

An' the next mornin' we was in eight fat'om o' water . . . an' that's not very much. Off o' Sable Island. We was on the nor'west bar then – eight fat'om o' water. An' we went acrost. Run 'er acrost the bar . . . why she didn't strike I don't know. My God, it was an awful sea. Worst I ever experienced. I never seen nothin' like that. Never in my life.

I thought we was all gone. I almost give up. An' the next mornin' . . . I didn't mind it till the next mornin' . . . till I went to take my oil clothes off. Then I got frightened. Boys, I broke down. I cried. An' the water . . . the tears just rolled down my cheeks. An' throwin' up . . . an' I kept throwin' up an' throwin' up.

The Cap'n an' the men cried an' hugged me when we got out of it. The Cap'n said, "If it wouldn't'a been for Carl, perhaps we'd'a been all gone."

An' it's strange how t'ings happen . . . Titus Baker from West Dublin an' Enos Baker – that was his son – they always went toget'er aboard of a vessel. They always slept toget'er in a double bunk. An' this year they separated an' Enos went wit' Cap'n John Mosher in the *Sylvia Mosher*, an' Titus, he went wit' us in the *Silver Thread*. We was to the west'ard o' the *Sylvia Mosher* an' we never seen 'er when we was out. But when we got in we heard she was lost an' all hands gone. Didn't know nothin' about it till we come home . . . an' they didn't return. An' when Titus heard it . . . he almost went crazy. Boys, he felt some bad.

My first trip that I made vessel fishin', it was in 1926, wit' Cap'n Jim Getson. I was only thirteen year old. I didn't go into a dory. I was a deck hand – takin' the heads off fish – header. An' that summer the fish was some plenty – my gracious the fish was numerous. An' the biggest kind.

Anyways, that was the summer that the August Gale was . . . that was the first big August Gale. An' we had a lot o' fish . . . had 'er pretty well filled up. An' this day . . . well, you couldn't hear anyt'in' about any storms – no radios. Just had your glass to go by – weather glass. An' the glass . . . the glass never showed not'in'. So this day was the sixth of August . . . day before the storm was – storm was the seventh. We fished in the mornin', but in the afternoon we never fished. There was no wind, but it was all a heavy swell runnin' – everyt'in' was not'in' but a big heavy swell. Late in the afternoon it was gettin' worse . . . battened all the hatches – covered everyt'ing o'er wit' tarpaulins. An' that evenin' I stood watch wit' the t'roater – that was our watch, from seven to nine. It was gettin' bad then. Before our watch was up everyt'in' began to spin around on the decks – everyt'in' began to . . . nothin' but awash. Seas comin' in o'er the deck . . . washin' the gear o'er board. That's how bad it was.

So sometime t'rough the night then we parted – parted the cable. An' had no sail. Couldn't get no sail on. Nothin' but the ridin' sail. An' we went all that night under bare poles . . . just lettin' 'er go. An' the next mornin' then, sometime in the mornin', got some sail on, managed to get some sail on. Oh my, oh my, the sea . . . was vicious. An' blowin'. It was wicked to the world – blowin', you. That was the biggest storm ever I was into.

An' sometime – this was on Sunday then, was onto a Sunday – sometime in the afternoon we got down into ten fat'oms o' water. We was driftin' down onto Sable Island. Hurricane o' wind. Look you, it was desperate. It hung on so long. The sea got so heavy – the wind blowin' the little seas down o'er the big ones . . . little seas crawlin' down o'er the big ones. An' the skipper's brother, he was mate wit' us an' he come down for'ard – in the fo'c's'le. All hands looked at him standin' in the doorway . . . just standin' there you.

"You got any friends home now," he said, "it's time to t'ink on 'em." He told us, "Get ready. Everybody stays on deck . . . I t'ink we're all hands gone. If she strikes the bar," he said, "every man for himself, the Devil for us all." Well, I'll never forget it. Some o' the men was layin' in their bunks. An' some of 'em said, "What's the good to go on deck? We might as well go here as on deck." So some of 'em went on deck, some of 'em never went on deck.

But . . . we must o' went across the bar – got out o' the shallow water. So anyway, after a while we begin to hit deeper water . . . an' then, after a long while we got into water quite deep. Well then, we knowed we was across the bar. Seas weren't breakin' so much, you understand.

An' that gale lasted . . . lasted all that night an' all the next day. An' it lasted all the next day comin'. My gracious it struck an' made t'ings stand around. I'm tellin' you. She was nothin' but awash . . . an' the vessel was deep you know, wit' fish.

Deep wit' a lot o' fish an' all awash. Lost a lot o' gear off the deck. But anyway . . . the wind after a while it died away. We left for home an' got home on the twelfth of August.

We didn't know anythin' about the other vessels bein' lost. In them times there was no way you could know. An' we didn't know till we got in off land – I t'ink it was down here off Cross Island. Was a lot o' shore boats there an' they come along side an' told us what happened. The *Sylvia Mosher* she went ashore – a sea struck 'er an' put 'er end o'er end. Split 'er right in two. She stood there for years . . . till she went under the sand. The *Sadie Knickle* – they never got no trace o' her. Sunk to her anchor, you. It wasn't very nice, I'm tellin' you . . . my father was in one of 'em an' my uncle an' my first cousin . . . they was lost in the *Sadie Knickle*. Fourteen gone from out home there in that storm . . . my father was the oldest. He was forty-two. An' the most of 'em was in their twenties. It was sad . . . knowed 'em all.

I was thirteen when I left on that trip – spent my fourteenth birthday there. Still kept goin'. Made a good many trips. It seemed like I was . . . I wanted to go.

That was fifty year ago this August. I was only a boy when my father was lost on the *Sadie Knickle* . . . an' Willard, my brother, he was out in the same storm wit' Cap'n Jim Getson. Willard got back . . . got saved, you. I remember where I was when the news come. Me an' my grandfather was up there off Halibut Head jiggin' squid. Used to go up there in the evenin's an' jig our bait for the next day. Well, there was no wind here . . . a big swell on, but no wind. We didn't know nothin' about it . . . It was soon time for 'em . . . for 'em to come home. The vessels would soon be loaded wit' fish.

We was up there that night – there was a lot o' boats there like there was every evenin', jiggin' squid. There's a feller, Robert Walfield was his name – he's dead now – an' he was up to Gordon's store. An' when he got up there why he found the news out. So he come right out an' he come right up there where we was jiggin' squid . . . because he knew that there was a lot o' the men out there. He t'ought he'd tell the whole story . . . what happened. He said, "The *Sylvia Mosher*, she lays ashore on Sable Island. All hands gone. An' the *Sadie Knickle*" – that's the one my father was in – "she's gone. Can't get no word on her." Well, that was the news. My father was into 'er, an' his brother, Robert. An' that was the first trip that Uncle Robert had his son wit' . . . Redwis . . . he was only young . . . fourteen, he was. Well, there was t'ree right from one house. An' my brother, Willard, he was on his first trip wit' Cap'n Getson – I can't remember the name o' the vessel any more – an' I guess he come close to gettin' lost. Got clear o' the island . . . . But down to the lower islands . . . John Bell was gone . . . Hastings Himmelman . . . Melvin Richards – that'd be Marion's brother . . . he was twenty. Then here was Guy Baker an' his brother Caleb . . . Caleb had his son, Blanchard wit' . . . just a boy, fifteen years old. Frank Walfield . . . Arthur Baker . . . Enos Baker . . . . An' then three men from Mount Pleasant that was born out here . . . an' . . . an' up in Blue Rocks, up past Lunenburg, there was upwards of forty men that was lost. That was a hard scratch. I know lots an' lots o' times I set down an' t'ink onto it. My father an' all them men . . . gone. The whole works of 'em.

An' from that on the LaHave Islands out there . . . it used to be . . . it was a dance an' somethin' goin' on there all the time. That storm killed the islands . . . it was just the same as somethin' come right down o'er the islands, you. You see, it was all young men that was drowned . . . all of 'em. Nobody felt like havin' dances or anythin' else wit' all our young people gone . . . we had no courage for anythin' like that. Everybody felt too bad about it. An' it . . . honest . . . it was never the same out there.

Well after them August Gales, it just seemed that . . . from then on vessel fishin' seemed to die out. I wouldn't just like to say that it was on account o' the August Gales that vessel fishin' died out. It could'a been somethin' like that . . . I don't know . . . after a while the men wouldn't go. They couldn't get a crew. I know I shipped one year wit' a feller . . . an' afterwards I dropped out. Next trip more of 'em left . . . he never got away a'tall . . . couldn't get a crew. It kept droppin' . . . kept droppin', droppin' . . . till they was all gone. An' they started to get these here draggers . . . draggers started to take over. Easier work, you understand. A lot o' vessels was sold up in Newfoundland an' a lot was lost. They was sold or lost. There's one yet up here in Lunenburg – the *Theresa E. Conner* – but she's only a museum. That's all that's left.

# At Least You Was Home

# I Growed Up Wit' Fishin'

We got married, Vera an' I got married in 1926. That's when the depression was. An' I went vessel fishin' four summers after that – after we was married – an' every summer it kept gettin' worse an' worse. After I was married, I was two years wit' Cap'n Dan Romkey winter an' summer, an' I was wit' him the next year then. Then I was wit' Cap'n Lee Lohnes, that was t'ree. An' all the time gettin' worse when you go to settle up. You would fetch home a load o' fish an' all the time goin' down, no money. An' the fourth year I was wit' Cap'n Lem Ritcey on t'ree trips out o' Riverport. An' we had twenty-four hundred quintals o' fish – that was on the summer trip. An' when we went down to settle in the fall, we made ninety-four dollars off o' that many fish . . . o'er two t'ousand quintals.

Well Bernie Wolf lived out on the Spe'tacles then, an' I heard tell he had a boat for sale. An' I went out an bought his boat . . . a double-ender she was. An' I said, "I'm goin' to try to do it on my own." For one summer, I only figured on one summer. I said, "Vera, I'm goin' to try it out myself for one summer." I went that summer an' I had eighty-seven quintals o' fish when fall come – dried cod fish – eighty-seven quintals. That was a big catch. An' when I had the salt paid for down to Riverport – you get your salt whenever you want it, an' not pay for it till fall – an' when I had everythin' squared up, I had forty-seven dollars clear from the summer. I tried it the next year 'cause it was no good to go vessel fishin' . . . you wouldn't make nothin'. An' fishin' off the shore here was the same way – but at least you was home. So I kept at it. I stayed home the first year there an' I kept on stayin' home. Never went back to vessel fishin' no more.

Most o' the fellers around here started fishin' wit' their fathers – shore fishin' – they all learned from their fathers, you know. I forget any more how old I was when . . . I know Dad, he put me in the boat an' rolled me up in a blanket . . . took me out. I used to fall asleep. But what I mean after a while I enjoyed it. I t'ought there was nothin' like it, you – goin' fishin'. I suppose it was good that way . . . at the time.

Well, Dad would give me a little money for the work I done wit' 'im an' I'd buy a net an' one t'ing and anot'er. An' then I started goin' by myself . . . bought my own boat when I was fifteen, you. An' I started gettin' involved wit' a whole lot o' fishin' gear . . . I growed up wit' fishin' . . . I growed damn well up wit' it. I'll say the word . . . an' it got so then to the point that it was pretty hard for me to back out 'cause I didn't want to lose what I had. But probably it would o' been a whole lot better if I would of. But I don't know . . . I been at this old game for fifty odd years. It's a long time . . . but when you're at it, it don't seem that long. Time goes around so fast that before you look around, one year's gone . . . the next year's back again. And you're at the same old story.

I know when I was just a boy – I'd say seven years old – my father would learn me how to knit twine for lobster traps. An' I started in at that age an' I was showed very little how to do it but I picked it right up just as soon as I got at it. Worked right along wit' my father, you see.

An' my father used to buy lobsters. What he had for to buy lobsters wit', he had a – if you ever remember a forty-cent bakin' powder can that held a pound. That's what he put his money in. Well the prices wasn't very much. You could buy a great big lobster then for five cents. We measured 'em wit' a stick we had wit' a piece o' tin onto it to mark for what we called nine-inch lobsters. Yes sir, t'ree cents for nine-inch lobsters an' five cents for the big ones. Not much of a price is it? Nothin's what I call it.

Anyway, as soon as I grew up an' my father didn't do that any more then I took over buyin' lobsters, you see. An' I carried the same t'ing to put my fortune in – a forty-cent bakin' powder can.

I lived out on the islands see, an' to get to school I had to eit'er sail or take the oars an' row. An' maybe sometimes I didn't go to school, you understand. Put the sail on that little red punt an' soak 'er out around the point. An' there I'd stay – put a line o'er an' catch some o' them little pollack. I t'ought fishin' was a little better'n school, you. But many times my father used to go after me – 'cause I was too small. He'd come after me, mind you, an' send me off to the school house. But that was the beginnin' of my fishin'.

Went fishin' when I should o' been in school. Didn't care about school . . . didn't know any better then. Might as well say it. 'Course once you get plenty of experience, well, that's sometimes more good to you than you get out of . . . in some t'ings . . . out of books. I just learned t'ings along wit' Dad. Then accordin' to a feller got older, why . . . learn different t'ings. You have to be at fishin' for quite a while before you know it . . . an' then you still don't quite ever really know everythin'.

But like I said there are some fellers that can really self-educate themselves in a lot o' different ways. Experiences are the best way in some t'ings . . . in fishing, yes. You can go in ashore, set in a school or somewhere, you know, like they do – the navigation school, but in the end, it's nothin' like experience. When you get out there on the ocean, get caught out there in a hurricane or somethin' like that, you won't be the same as what you were studyin' out of a book. It's a different story all together.

⚓

A lot o' people come around here . . . an' you'll always hear the story of the stupid fishermen. This I've heard time an' time again. It goes years back, you know. And yet there is a lot o' people that t'ink it yet. Well, I'll admit there's not too many of us got too much education. I mean we can't talk to educated people. But you take most o' the fishermen now, somethin' happens to their boats, they can fix 'em, quite a lot o' the fishermen can build their own boats an' if they want a house, they build it, fish store or anyt'ing they go ahead an' well . . . do it. An' this was the best education they could get . . . was to do it themselves.

⚓

I didn't have no choice. I had to leave school. I graded for the sixth grade. I was in the fifth grade an' I graded for the sixth then. An' I'm goin' to tell you my dear man, today they might have a lot of education, a lot of 'em but I still can beat 'em – a lot of 'em. It sounds foolish but it's a fact. When I got a big job to do . . . maybe it'd be days or maybe weeks before I got that done. Then I can set down an' t'ink, "I'm some glad that I got it done." It makes me feel some happy . . . about what I got done, see – not like workin' in one o' them educated jobs, you.

The young generation wants to be all educated. They don't want to go to fish. They want that everybody was educated an' all have fancy jobs. Well, I got a job I ain't ashamed of. An' I'm t'inkin' the time's goin' to come – it's comin' fast – that it's goin' to be no one left to fish. A lot, they don't want to go fishin' . . . they want somethin' else . . . always somethin' else. It's goin' to happen that way. An' it's goin' to make it bad. There's a time comin' – like I heard a feller sayin' – it will be no fishin' an' no farmers. When the time comes for the table to be set . . . there'll be nothin' to eat on the table. Well that's a fact.

There's a lot o' the younger people today that has been educated . . . educated to their finger ends. An' they got big jobs . . . they ain't too fussy about bein' very friendly wit' fishermen. Right around our own back door that happened to us. You see you're in wit' the bigger shots an' more money. I don't like that. I know fishin' is a hard life. I know that. You're goin' t'rough an awful lot o' hard weat'er an' you have some darn hard days an' hard hours. You take a lot of punishment. It's a hard life. That it is. My whole life I've spent fishin' an' takin' everythin' into account . . . well, you feel good while you're goin' at it . . . but then sometimes you t'ink maybe you don't amount to nothin'. There is ups an' downs . . . like anythin' I guess. It's all in a lifetime, all in a lifetime.

Well, this here shore fishin' is reachin' its end. The young fellers is leavin' an' when they're gone it ain't goin' to start up again. Don't matter how many fish comes around . . . it's reachin' its end. 'Cause to learn all the tricks o' the trade, it's somet'in' you have to grow up wit'. Then you know somet'in' about it. You learn from little on up. But, y'know, somebody new to start, it's a little more to it than you t'ink. You take steamin' off here twenty odd miles in black t'ick o' fog an' findin' your buoys an' then gettin' back – you got to use a lot o' judgement. Say you're runnin' off here, off here from the Gas Buoy an' there's a tide runnin'. You might have a course nor'west an' the tide is runnin' to the west'ard. Well in a mile or two you'd never believe how much the tide is goin' to take you out o' your course. You've got to allow a half a point or a point off from the compass readin'. An' the same t'ing comin' back – you got to take into account the tide an' the wind. I learned quite a bit from my father. An' then, y'know, I learned a lot on my own. When you grow up wit' it, you learn a little every day, every year. What I'm sayin' . . . once the younger fellers are gone off there won't be no one takin' it up again. That'll be the end o' this old racket, you.

# A Beautiful Long Day

Dad told me about goin' fishin' off the shore here years ago. They used to row from here off to the Stone Wall. They used to leave t'ree, four o'clock in the mornin' wit' a pair of oars – started off here in the oil ca'm an' sail back if the wind breezed up some. An' if it didn't come no wind, they had to row all that distance back in again. An' then he said they'd get home an' he'd have some fish – they dressed an' salted their fish in them days. An' some nights – if they had any amount o' fish – they never got to bed. They lay on the floor o' the stage till the next mornin'. It was hard work. There's no two ways about it. They worked hard . . . they all worked hard in them days. It's no good to say they didn't.

When I was eight, I went wit' my grandfather. I remember, my mother, she made me a suit of oil clothes – an' oiled 'em. Them was my outfit . . . an' I had a pair o' rubber boots. We had no boat wit' an engine . . . he always rowed. Oh, we done some rowin' in them days. We went off, I suppose, about ten or twelve miles to what they called the Stone Wall. Outside the shore soundin's. An' that's where we fished. An' maybe have to row home if no wind come. Look, I'm goin' to tell you wit' some people's boats – you might t'ink I'm exaggeratin' but it's the truth – them t'warts was wored down from settin' onto 'em an' rowin'. That's right . . . an' some, well my grandfather an' some o' them would have a – your oil pants wouldn't stand it settin' on the t'wart – you'd have an extra patch in the oil pants put on the seat part for to keep 'em from wearin' t'rough when you was rowin'. An' then you'd paint 'em yet an' make 'em harder. It was hard work – rowin'.

I remember when they got the first motors into boats around here. Yes, that's quite a while ago. Our fellers o'er there on the Kingsburg side, when they talked about gettin' these boats wit' engines in 'em . . . they seen all the fellers, you know, around the islands – they got 'em before o'er there. Well some of 'em they'd sit around there talkin', sayin', "Well now, what will you do if you come in and you want to stop one o' these here engines? You mightn't get 'er stopped! They're such funny t'ings, you know." But the whole trouble was when we got engines – the trouble was to get 'em started! They'd stop themselves.

Why, some fellers'd have engines . . . they wouldn't use 'em. They'd row 'em around. Frightened to use 'em. I know one feller that he had an engine till he gave up fishin', an' there was a person bought it afterwards – it was just the same as a brand new engine. Well, in all my time, I don't believe that I seen that engine goin' a dozen times – his boat, always rowin' or sailin'. Now that was some sense to that! I wished different times somebody would go over in the night an' smash the row locks off. That's right!

At one time I went shore fishin' day an' night. Now on Sunday – I didn't go fishin' on Sunday – I waited till after twelve o'clock . . . you know, on Sunday night . . . which I call tomorrow. And when I come in I had more fish than the other fellers. That means that you work all night, you . . . you don't work just in the daytime. And no man I don't t'ink . . . they . . . when I'd come into the cold storage they would say, "There, here comes – the iron man." That's what they called me. See I was alone . . . always. When two men went, I went. It didn't make any matter. I fished alone an' I fished hard.

Well, shore fishin', fishin' off the shore here . . . I call it a day an' a half. Get up anywheres on from two o'clock in the mornin'. Get up an' leave – I don't eat too much breakfast in the mornin' . . . very seldom. Maybe a cup o' coffee or somet'in'. But I eat then on the way out. See, it takes time when you set down an' eat. You can eat goin' out . . . do two t'ings at once. You can be steamin' an' eatin' an' you're gettin' that much more ahead – closer to the fishin' ground. Spend an hour or an hour an' a half steamin' off to your nets. Get out there an' haul your nets . . . have maybe twenty-five, thirty nets to look after. An' then if you're puttin' trawl out you set that. From there you go out an' anchor somewheres an' fish on the handline till maybe four or five in the afternoon. Come in an' dress fish an' run 'em o'er to the plant to sell 'em. An' if it's a long evenin' in the summer you'll come down to the building – there's always t'ings to do. You got twine to work at . . . mendin' nets . . .

NATHAN S. JOUDREY & SON LTD.
Phone (Area Code 902) MAHONE BAY 624-8462
JANUARY
1972
DENVER
SNACK

7up
G.S. MAYO
GENERAL STORE

first
against
thirst

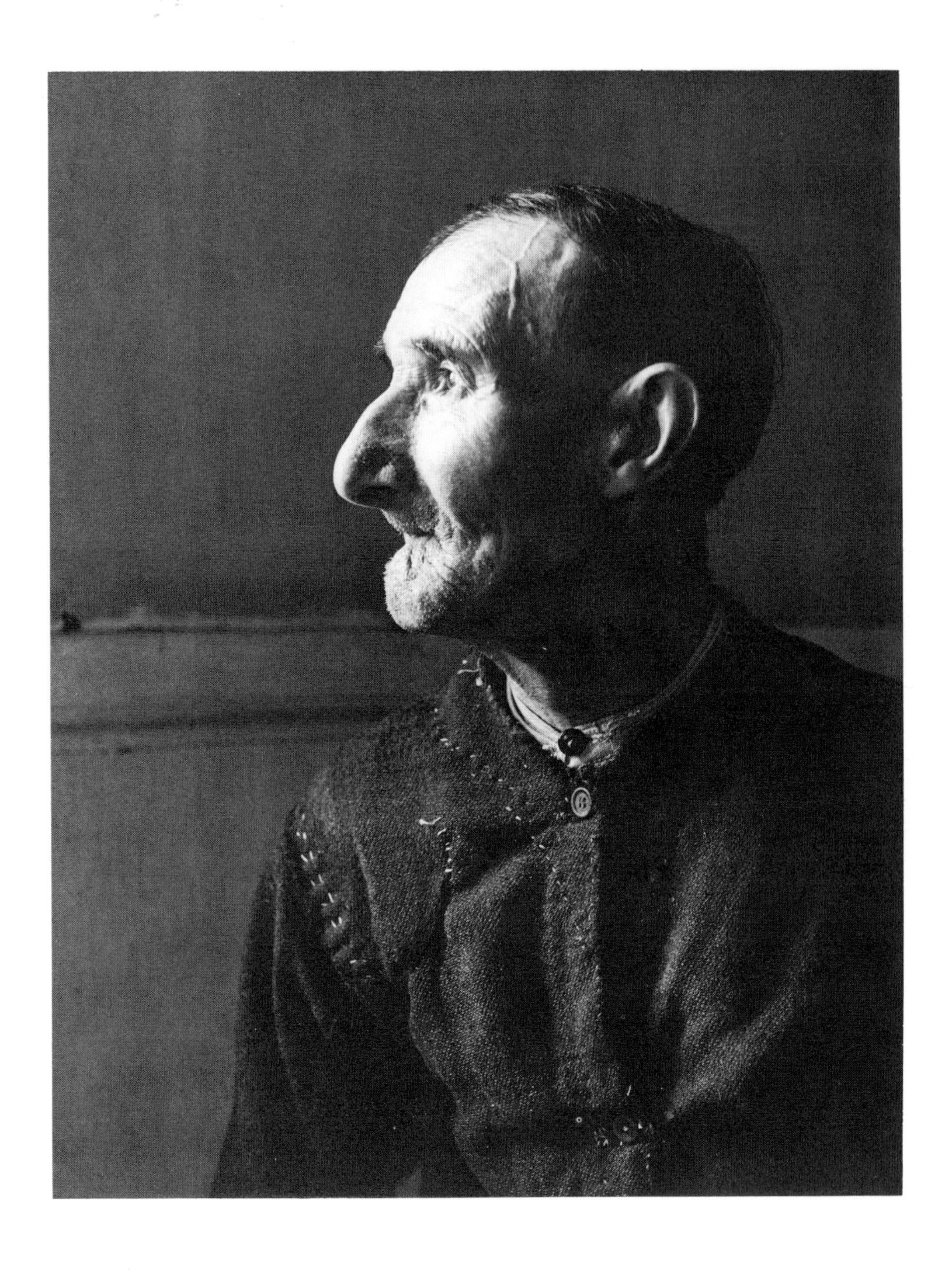

there's always somethin' around the boat to do. One t'ing an' anot'er. You can keep yourself right happy all day long. You don't lose too many hours – one feller alone has got his hands full. It makes a beautiful long day.

There's one t'ing about fishin' . . . there's always somethin' new to try an' you're always in the want of somethin' thinkin', "Well, I'm goin' to do better." Now lots o' times it pans out to be better an' sometimes it doesn't, but then if that don't pan out there'll be somethin' else come up. There seems to be somethin' always to excite you . . . you know, to help you get a little bit more encouraged into it. You always got a little somethin' to keep you . . . to start it up again.

'Course sometimes it gets awful discouragin' . . . you often t'ink to yourself, "This I got to give up. I can't stand it no longer." It can disgust you so bad. Sometimes you get into a bad storm an' lose, maybe, t'ree parts o' the gear you got out . . . you'll grumble to yourself. It sets you back some. But then it seems there's always somethin' that makes you go back at it again.

I know one spring, an' that wasn't so very many springs ago, I had seventy-five traps out. Come a big storm . . . it lasted for quite a few days till we got out. An' what do you t'ink I had left out of seventy-five? I had twenty-four pieces in all . . . out of seventy-five good traps. An' I said to Marion, I said, "I'm settin' no more traps this spring. If I set any more, I won't have none for fall."

I had quite a little bit o' damage done home there around the wharves an' slip from the storm. So I said, "I'm givin' it up, an' I'm goin' to do some work around home." I fixed up my slip. Went in the woods an' cut poles an' stuff, an' fixed up the wharf. An' after a while I got this done. An' you know, it used to bother me. One day I said to Marion, I said, "I can't do this. I got to set – if I lose 'em or whatever, I got to set some traps."

It was onto a Saturday . . . I'll never forget it. Was onto a Saturday. I took fifty more out . . . an' set 'em. An' the next day was Sunday. Well, here o'er the radio they give the weather out . . . storm comin' wit' forty to fifty mile winds. Well I knowed what that meant. Listen, I never fished on Sunday in my life – that's somethin' I never done. But if I could save anythin', had anythin' out for to save . . . I went for to try to save it. So I said to Marion, "Sunday or no Sunday," I said, "get me some breakfast. I'm goin' out an' I'm bringin' them traps in." So I hauled the fifty of 'em on the boat, an' brought 'em in – shifted 'em here to the inside o' Mosher's Harbour. Get 'em out o' the heavy seas, you understand. I don't know how long they laid there. It stormed, kept stormin' . . . stormin'. An ' they was smashed to pieces – an' some was gone altoget'er.

Well that set me back, you. It makes hard work . . . you're all the time at it. A lot o' work to it. A lot o' hard work to it. Sometimes you just can't win . . . always on the losin' end.

I was goin' fishin' in a double-ender at the time. And I turned out at t'ree o'clock this mornin' an' went out an' picked my nets. I just had enough herrin' for bait – a basket or two full of herrin'. Well I went off to a place we call the Big Shoal to try for some ground fish on the handline. It was oil ca'm an' I never shifted all day – I just laid still. I was gettin' some haddock an' some codfish among 'em. I spent my whole day there.

An' I had all my bait used, mind you, but just one herrin'. Well, a herrin' belly is the best t'ing for bait, you understand. You just cut the belly off right straight an' put a split into the end of it. I done that an' I put that down – my last piece o' bait, mind you. Listen, it wasn't no sooner down when this t'ing grabbed it. And boys, I pulled on it, an' the line she cracked. But he laid right still . . . he never moved. And I knew it had to be a halibut – the way it laid . . . an' it wasn't that close to the bottom that the hook was hooked in the bottom. Had anot'er line o'er board – had to get that up. I had to haul wit' one hand and hold this other – see I didn't know the minute he might take off an' if I didn't hold 'im, why he'd' a just broke free an' that's all I'd 'a seen of 'im. And 'course the grapplin' was o'erboard. A big halibut like that – if he got fouled . . . snarled up in the moorin' line, it's gone for sure. Well, I couldn't haul that up – t'ought I'd take a chance on it.

Well, I grabbed my gob stick an' my gaff an' my halibut napper an' all the t'ings I needed – right there close. 'Case I did happen to get 'im up. An' after a while he started to come, but not fast – he wasn't anyways fussy about it a'tall, just come easy. An' I kept lookin' o'erboard an' lookin' o'erboard an' lookin' o'erboard, an' after a while boys, he started to go again like lightnin', for the bottom – right straight down. I had a line an' a half on the rail on account of a halibut – everybody does. But if he'd'a went off to the side I'd'a lost 'im – not enough line see. Well, he went straight to the bottom an' I had a hard job to start 'im off again mind you. An' he done it again an' then again – he done it three times. But the third time I kept watchin' for 'im. I seen his mouth was open, an' boys, his mouth looked big enough to shove a bucket down. Oh boy, there was a size he was!

I kept soakin' at 'im, an' every once in a while he'd get them shakes you know, an' I t'ought to myself, "Old feller, I believe you're pretty well done in. You're t'rough old boy." The way he was workin' I knowed . . . anyway I kept soakin' 'im up an' soakin' 'im up an' boys when his nose broke out o' the water I give it to 'im. I gave 'im t'ree or four wacks right on the end o' the nose wit' the halibut napper. I grabbed the gaff an' soaked it right in his eye. Well, I looked at my fish . . . I t'ought to myself, "I'm afraid, old fish, I won't get you in the boat. But I'm goin' to try." I t'ought o' towin' 'im in – or hollerin' to my brother Calvin. His boat layed not too far off. The two of us could o' hauled him in, see. But I wanted to try it an' see what I could do.

Well, I shifted my fish boxes – the haddock an' cod – an' the gear o'er to his side, see. Listed 'er o'er on the one side, an' I tried 'im . . . but the first time I couldn't come it. His mouth was so open an' I had to hold 'im so far off o' the boat before I had his head clear . . . see it made an awful pull. But boys oh boys, the next time I stood right up on a fish crate. And I give 'im an extra pull. Boys, I give 'im an extra tug an' he come right in o'er the water board an' went for'ard – bursted my bulk head an' everyt'in' – his nose went right in the bow. He only made t'ree or four slaps, that's all he made, little slaps.

That's all he had left into 'im, you.

I walked for'ard an' I cut my hook out'a him – the hook I had in my line, an' I hauled my halibut hook out'a him and I reeled everyt'ing up an' I went right for'ard an' got my grapplin' up. I never hesitated at all after that. I give it to 'er for in.

Well I got right down by the breakwater an' Mr. Reinders he come out – the owner. He was a great big man, oh he was a tidy man – he always had his collar an' tie on. He come out onto the wharf an' looked down o'er it an' he says, "What in the name o' God you got there?" An' they all started to come out in there – the fellers in the shed. He yelled, "How in the name o' God we goin' to get that up on the wharf?"

"Oh," I says, "you'll get it up on the wharf all right. All I want is a good piece o' rope. All I got here in the boat is small stuff. You got a piece o' fifteen t'read or eighteen t'read – somet'in' like that?"

"Yes," he said, "I'll give you a piece o' rope. But I can't get 'im up alone an' neither can you. That's goin' to be a nice little pull."

Well, I got the rope fast an' I says, "Now," I says, "you can bend onto that!" An' Murdock was there an' George an' Eldred an' this other feller, Mr. Cross an' Mr. Reinders – the owner – he was there wit' his white shirt on. It wasn't white when he was t'rough! There was a lot o' men there – an' they got to work . . . an' they walked 'im up onto the wharf.

Some said he was t'ree hundred pound, some said two hundred an' fifty . . . an' all that there. I t'ought, "I ain't goin' to say nothin' 'cause I don't know."

Murdock he looked at me an' says, "How much does he weigh?"

I says, "I don't know . . . I can't tell you. But he's goin' to weigh heavy. All's I can say is I ain't goin' to catch these every year – this is the biggest one an' the only big one I ever caught in my life."

Well we got 'im weighed an' he weighed two hundred an' sixty-eight – wit' the head off an' gutted. Two hundred an' sixty-eight . . . dressed.

They wouldn't believe I hauled 'im in alone. I tried it an' I done it. An' they wouldn't believe me, mind you! No sir, they wouldn't believe that I hauled 'im in alone!

Oh, he was a big fish an' a nice fish.

I got started at it when I was twelve an' here I am . . . sixty-four this next October comin'. It got into my blood an' it'd be hard to get away. Hard to get away, you . . . must be born into me. I don't know, it's . . . you know what a weed is like on the ground . . . it'll still grow an' grow. Well, I t'ink that's the way it is when you're . . . when you're startin' to go to sea. Because there's somethin' about it that . . . I don't know, you get . . . . You can't leave it. I don't know what I'd do if I had to walk away from it. If I got somewheres where I couldn't see water I don't know what would happen. If I got up in the mornin' an' couldn't see water . . . . Might as well kill me you, an' be done wit' it. I'm so long out I don't t'ink I could stand bein' closed in all day. I don't like it in a town or city . . . a buildin' where it's all dusty an' whatever. I want to see the water . . . an' the good clear air.

An' when you come to t'ink on it us fellers got a lot that other fellers ain't. Now, you take up to the Michelin plant . . . you got to go stand there for eight hours. If you're into a place where you put six bolts in as everyt'in' comes along . . . you do that today an' you do it the next day . . . an' every second or every minute, however long it takes you . . . an' look a'here, it must get terrible on a feller. Why all a feller'd look for . . . eight in the mornin' you'd start. An' then look for twelve o'clock – come an' get your dinner, an' then from twelve o'clock, look for five to quit. Somebody comin' along sayin', "Well, now you do this," or "do somet'in' else." At home . . . well, you might work from daylight till dark an' you don't t'ink not'in' of it. When you're workin' for yourself, why you're workin' to get the job done. You ain't t'inkin' on the time. Ain't workin' for somebody else. Somebody else payin' you, why you ain't lookin' to get the work done . . . just get the hours in.

An' as far as somebody bossin' me around, I don't have that. I can do my own bossin'. That's worth a lot sometimes.

When I first went at it – turn out before daylight an' steam out here when it's t'ick o' fog or dirty – you know, loppy an' like'a that. That was my glory then. You see, fishin' on these shoals outside here – we got marks for all these shoals. Well if it was a fine day there'd be not'in' but a mass o' boats there. But if it was t'ick o' fog, black t'ick o' fog, there wouldn't be hardly any boats on them places. They couldn't find 'em – every feller couldn't find 'em, you.

I had everyt'in' put down, you understand – the points o' the compass an' how many minutes it would take me. There's a place called the Ridge – the Little Ridge we called it – oh, it's out from the rock, east sou'east from Black Rock there. An' I used to go up to Black Rock there – where the boats used to lay if it was dirty. An' I would just keep on goin'. When I got close to the rock I'd steam'er off. East sou'east, so many minutes. Left the other fellers behind, you.

And now! If somebody was to say to me in the mornin', "Go up – steam up to Black Rock an' give it to 'er off in black t'ick fog or blowin', "I'd say, "you're crazy." No courage left, you.

If I live to see the twentieth of April, I'll be seventy-nine, you. What I do now, I don't call it fishin'. I keep at the work a bit – set a few nets, just to pass the time away. Four or five nets – that's not'in' you. An' when it comes t'ick o' fog – in the mornin's when it's t'ick o' fog, I don't go off fishin' nowheres you.

I guess it must be the age creepin' up on a feller . . . if I'd'a kept young it wouldn't'a been so bad.

# You Never Think on Fear

Listen, when your time is here, you're goin', that's it. It don't matter where it is, what you're doin', how old you are, or how young you are. When that day is called, that's your end. I can't see it no other way. 'Course death is sad whenever it strikes. It's sad. But it's no good to think on dyin' or fear it . . . . You never think on fear. If you thought about that, if you had that in your mind all the time I don't think you'd make anythin' of yourself. Whenever your time is, that's it. They say that's not right – it's foolishness. But I say it is right. That's the way I size the whole thing up.

One o' the worst t'ings I always t'ink about in this shore fishin' . . . when it's t'ick o' fog an' there's a ground sea on the shore. Not a wind lop, but a ground sea. When you're runnin' in – when you're off here an hour or two – why, if you don't make where you take a course for comin' in . . . if you make to the east'ard or west'ard, you're in shoal water. I dread that. You've got to try to get in close enough on the shore for to see the land, you know, to tell where you are. An' I'll tell you, sometimes when there's a ground sea on, it's not one o' the best t'ings . . . if it ever would break on you . . . . It don't give you a very nice feelin' t'inkin' about it.

Like out here once . . . Dad used to tend the light out there to Mosher's Head. An' one day . . . it was after a southerly . . . there was a Cape Island boat drifted down past there. Had two men in – their engine broke down. They drifted down that mornin' past Black Rock. Heavy sea on, y'know after the storm – an' low tide. Yes sir, it was heavy . . . it was dirty. Dad an' I saw them an' we towed their boat in there by the lighthouse, in the cove. Two fellers from around Lunenburg. Boys, they didn't . . . after they got ashore there, the one feller . . . I guess you don't mind it so much at first, but, you know, it took a'hold of him. He was right shaky like . . . they come awful close to Black Rock. I know it must o' give 'em an awful feelin' comin' in. Their anchor line parted an' they couldn't do nothin'.

I can just picture somethin' like that . . . 'cause how many times a feller was out at his nets or fishin' in a storm an' if anythin' went wrong . . . . It'd give you quite a feelin'. I'll tell you that.

The trouble of it is when you go out there it's all dangerous. You go off from the land a piece of ways. An' the first t'ing the fog'll shut down or somet'in' an' then you run for the land an' you're almost in against the shore an' it's rough . . . it's all dangerous. Any little t'ing could happen to the engine an' that's the end. I met that more than once. Not once, but more than once. An' plenty different times like that, you know.

I was almost drownded here off o' Ironbound. In the spring o' the year . . . after a big storm. Went ashore on Ironbound. I had traps there an' the sea had 'em all scattered around. I don't know why . . . you'd do more for a lobster trap than most anyt'in' else. You'll venture for one. Why I don't know. So I got some of 'em – hauled 'em right in the boat. Put fresh bait onto 'em an' said to myself, "I'll go in an' set these out an' then I'll come out an' fix some more up – take 'em in." I t'ink I only had one or two o'erboard. An' when I t'rowed the buoy for one o' them it went back an' jammed in the rudder an' the blades. I wasn't very far from the shore . . . had to go right close there for lobsters. An' it give me no chance a'tall. First t'ing I knowed I was ashore. Went right up on a sunken reef. An' it was quite a sea on . . . it used to come in an' t'row 'er almost down so her washboard'd be in the water. Well I said, "This is it." It was no good for me to jump . . . I t'ought about it . . . it was no good for me to jump out o' the boat 'cause I couldn't save myself. Slippery rock . . . right slanted an' the seas poundin' in there. So I t'ought to myself, "Now, this is it."

Well Gilbert, he was off from me an' he seen me. An' he come in. An' the first time . . . he could o' been in a mess too, tryin' to save me. An' the first time he come in he couldn't get me. So the next time, he come in across the reefs . . . he struck his boat comin' in across the reef. An' that time he got a rope to me. An' by luck, he pulled me off . . . off out o' there. If it wouldn't'a been for Gilbert, why that would'a been the end o' me . . . there wasn't anot'er boat around anywhere.

But I went back again . . . an' finished up my traps, the same day. I don't know . . . it didn't really frighten me at the time. But afterwards you t'ink about them t'ings.

I was about fourteen years old an' I'd been fishin' wit' my father a number o' years. An' we were out at our herrin' nets an' fishin' on the handlines . . . an' fish wasn't very plenty. So I wasn't catchin' any fish. I got kind o' tired of it . . . laid down to go to sleep. An' my father decided for to shift to a different place. He went up on the bow o' the boat to unfasten the line. An' the first t'ing, his feet slipped an' he went o'erboard. I jumped right up quick – I heard him when he fell in the water – an' I grabbed him for to haul him in the boat. Well, I wasn't a very big boy at the time . . . an' he was pretty heavy. He used to wear them boot bands around his boots to hold his oil pants tight. An' the water couldn't get out o' the oil clothes – between the rubber boots an' the oil pants. An' they was filled. He didn't have much faith in gettin' in the boat . . . an' there was nobody within miles from where we was.

Anyway, I held fast to 'im an' wit' his help, an' me pullin' . . . well, I got 'im in after a little. He was pretty well gone y'know, 'cause he was a man up in his fifties at that time. We left an' come home instead o' goin' out fishin' any farther. I managed to save him. I come pretty close to bein' the head o' the family that time. He often mentioned about it . . . y'know, from time to time afterwards . . . y'know, about me savin' him. It was a pretty close call . . . the risk is always there, you.

My father, Cale, is one o' the oldest . . . one o' the oldest lobster fishermen there is around. He still goes . . . he'll be ninety-three next birthday. He's pretty fresh lookin' yet . . . he's pretty lively. He goes in his boat alone – and hauls his own traps. Hauls by hand too, seventy-five, maybe a hundred traps. Don't use a hauler. All by hand. He's got good grit. He plans to go at 'er anot'er winter again. He talks about makin' a few traps extra for anot'er winter an' knittin' headin's an' one t'ing or anot'er. The grit's really there. Sometimes I t'ink he shouldn't be out . . . but then if somethin' does happen to 'im . . . well, he'll be at somethin' he likes.

I was out this one mornin' an' a ragin' thunder storm came up. Chased me in you – I went to work in my building. Old Cecil come down in time an' asked if I t'ought he could go out. Wanted to tend to his nets.

"Well," I said, "you can go out but you don't want to stay out. It's comin' back." I knowed it would.

"I'll only go to the near shoal," he said. He t'ought he wouldn't go in the both places where he had his nets.

But when he was t'rough wit' the first one, he did go in the second place an' I was workin' in the buildin' an' the first t'ing I t'ought the roof would come in. Everythin' was lit up. I knowed what that was. I ran out to see about Cecil.

He was on his way in – sailin' in. An old gaff rig he had. Sail up an' headed for shore. But I didn't see no man. I let out a yell, "Man either o'erboard or dead!" An' there was two other men down here. They took a boat then an' went to meet this one. They found Cecil on the floorboards an' brought him ashore. And the only t'ing that I could see on him was he had a mark back o' his one ear about the size of a twenty-five cent piece. But it was enough . . . to kill him.

They carried him up to the house in a hand barrow.

Nelse was down here on the day he got drownded. I was on vacation an' he was down here to the light station – Mosher's Head light. The assistant was talkin' to 'im here an' he left an' went home an' he got his supper an' he said he was goin' to West Dublin. I remember the night – it was a cool night . . . it was moonlight an' . . . really lovely night. An' up by Covey's Island . . . he struck Seal Rock up there.

Roy an' Lorraine, they were comin' out that next mornin' to go out to their nets, an' they saw the jigger mast o' Nelse's boat stickin' out o' the water. An' they went up an' looked an' they could see 'er layin' down on the bottom. She was in I suppose about ten or twelve feet o' water. Anyway they went o'er to his house an' they went up an' the house was all closed up. Nobody around . . . so they went on out to their nets. An' then when they come in, why, they started to inquire to find out, you know, if he was home or . . . they t'ought maybe, that his boat sunk an' somebody picked 'im up. But . . . but, that wasn't the case.

Lorraine an' I was out to our nets that mornin' an' we knowed he was gone when we got back. I took the doctor an' the Mounties out there . . . an' right to this day I still can't t'ink that man had to go in that kind of a way. That man understood boats an' he understood water an' everyt'ing else when it came to that part of it . . . so whatever happened, happened I t'ink, before he got there. Accordin' to what the doctor said, somethin' did come acrost 'im. Look, it was just as clear o'erhead . . . that was a dangerous rock. There was a big hole smashed in the bow o' the boat . . . as a matter o' fact there was t'ree into her. She just kept hittin' the rock . . . he never shut the engine off . . . 'cause the switch wasn't off. She just kept runnin' up against that rock.

He never put up any battle . . . I helped take 'im out o' the water. When the divers went down an' got 'im, I helped take 'im into my boat. An' when we took 'im out, why he never . . . his glasses was on his face an' he set just the same as settin' on a chair. He would o' been settin' on his engine box, see . . . an' he was settin' there wit' the tiller lines in his hands like he was steerin', you . . . so whatever . . . somethin' took 'im before he hit the rock.

We put 'im in the boat there an' rolled 'im in the canvas. It was weeks after . . . that I could still see 'im in my mind. It wore away after a while.

I guess he was goin' to West Dublin . . . I heard 'im go in, an' you know we always . . . always heard 'im come home if he was out. We didn't hear 'im come home . . . didn't hear 'im come home that night. Anyway, next mornin' it was, you, I went to my mackerel nets. I was goin' to my mackerel nets an' I didn't see Nelse's boat. An' a funny feelin' come o'er me, I talked to myself, I said, "Somethin's happened to Nelse." 'Cause when Nelse went anywhere he always was the man to be back home . . . wit' the dory hauled up on the slip. An' Nelse's dory lay off to the mooring. I said, "Somethin's happened."

I'd been out to the mackerel nets . . . an' first t'ing Roy an' Lorraine come an' said about Nelse bein' drownded. He struck Seal Rock . . . such a big hole into 'er that she sunk right away, right to the bottom . . . an' they found 'im right by the boat, you.

He always used to come o'er to our place a lot . . . lived by himself, you understand. Next day . . . I know he told us he was goin' to bring us – well, it was his birthday an' our wedding anniversary. He was bringin' us o'er a drink. An' the scotch . . . next day, the scotch stood there on the table in his house.

Yes, Nelse Risser made a bad . . . a bad endin' of it. He went up t'rough there all his life I guess . . . up an' down t'rough there. Rock tore the bottom out of 'er. You get in some bad messes sometimes if you've spent your whole lifetime fishin'. I wouldn't want to get in the messes I dreamed of already. I don't know how many times I dreamed that I sank . . . the sea broke onto me. I just dreamed it . . . but when I woke up I was some hot.

# The Future Ain't Good

Now, as far back as I can remember, fishin' was about all a feller could do. My father fished an' his father before him. They was onto the vessels o' course . . . both started off as boys. Then Dad, when he started in fishin' off the shore here . . . well, I learnt from him. I went wit' him, you understand, until . . . until I could go off on my own. I was, I guess thirteen when I had my own boat. See, fishin' was somet'in' you had to do . . . there really was no other choice. But y'know it's kind o' funny . . . there wasn't too many fellers I know of that didn't like it. You never t'ought that you was bein' pushed into anyt'in' . . . I guess if a feller would o' known any different . . . why I guess then he might o' seen other t'ings to do an' . . . . Well, like most o' the fellers around here – the young fellers, why, they're lookin' for to do other t'ings. Shore fishin' looks very bad. Looks very bad.

An' I'll tell you what's makin' it bad. Too many draggers is on the go . . . they got the bottom ruined. That's killin' the fishin' around here. A lot o' these fish feed off o' the bottom. An' a lot o' the bottom is like our land here – it's got all kinds o' weeds on the bottom. An' the fish eat the weeds. Like on a trawl when you're fishin' – once in a while you'll haul up a stone an' it'll have a little red berry onto it – looks like a strawberry. We used to call it a strawberry – a sea strawberry. Fish'll eat 'em. Well, when you're draggin' on the bottom, you drag up rocks, you drag up everyt'in' that's on the bottom – fish, lobsters. Now how much do you kill an' how much do you smash up? Fish can't stand it. No.

If I had a son that wanted to fish I'd tell 'im, "No boy. Go get a job an' no matter what kind o' job it is, go take it. Don't you ever start fishin'. For it's not goin' to last." That's how t'ings has changed . . . it's come to that.

I t'ink it's got a little bit too modern. If fishin' would o' been like in the old hook an' line days, I don't t'ink we would have so many problems. But I'm afraid . . . it seems that there's not near the fish on the shore that it used to be. I believe I caught in one week years back what I caught all last summer. Mind you, in summers past you could look at the boats comin' in an' make a good guess o' the weight o' fish the feller had just by the look of his boat . . . the way she set in the water. But now the seiners got the herrin' all done up . . . one o' them seiners, they take more right in one seine than all the shore boats do along here for a whole summer. T'ousands an' t'ousands an' t'ousands o' tons in just a few sweeps. An' it seems a shame what they done . . . ground 'em up for fish meal an' one thing or anot'er . . . that seems just a waste o' food to me. See, we have certain mesh nets that we fish an' the little ones we never get a'tall – they swim right t'rough there an' they stay alive. Them big seiners – they take everyt'ing. An' draggers is the same . . . .

I really t'ink that if they stayed wit' vessel fishin' like it was . . . fish wit' a hook an' line, I don't t'ink there'd be a shortage o' fish. But it seems now, they're just takin' 'em too fast. The ocean in times to come will get right fished out . . . emptied right out.

In them vessels we didn't have no fancy gear to find the fish. Go out to The Banks there an' shift around till we laid a'top o' some fish. The only t'ing we had to go by was the bottom. Carried a deep sea lead – them big leads, oh, as big around as your arm – you know for takin' a sound. Many a time we soaked 'er back off there on them vessels – them big leads. Had a hole in the end there filled wit' soap. You see, you let that go down an' it bounced up an' down on the bottom an' you could tell if you were on mud bottom, on sand bottom, or hard bottom. See if the soap was all plastered o'er wit' mud or filled wit' sand you could tell what kind of a bottom you were on. That's how we used to find the rocky bottom for to anchor on to catch fish. You couldn't get no fish on a mud bottom, you understand. That deep sea lead was only invented by a fisherman. That was a good rig . . . it done the job.

'Course a lot o' fellers'd say that was a backwards way o' doin' t'ings. Now on these draggers here they can look down in them machines an' see the fish swimmin' around. That's the reason they got the good part of 'em caught up. Too much lookin' for 'em – fish have no escape. They're draggin' off here the year round, twenty-four hours around the clock, t'ree hundred an' sixty-five days a year. An' wit' a dragger, you have these iron chains like . . . an iron net – all big iron links toget'er. I forget any more how many tons one o' them weighs. That's poundin' on the bottom . . . scrapin' the bottom like that. They're goin' to clean everyt'in' up after a while. See wit' dory fishin' off the vessels an' wit' these fellers in the shore boats, them that would bite on the hook . . . well you get them. An' the little ones get clear, see. But these draggers go off here an' drag t'rough them little ones . . . they go down right o'er the spawnin' ground. Why, they destroy 'em before they get big enough to swim! Destroy half again as many as they take . . . they're killin' everyt'in' . . . an tearin' the bottom to pieces. The bottom just can't stand it an' the fish can't stand it. They're goin' to clean everyt'in' up after a while. Be nothin' I guess for nobody. That's somethin' today I can't get wise to. It just don't make no sense to me.

It's gettin' worse every year. An' I'm expectin' to see the day, if it keeps goin', within the next ten years I'll say – an' that's givin' it a long time – that a feller'd have a hard job to go out here an' catch one for to eat. It's a darn shame. That's what I call it.

I never wanted Ernest to go fishin' . . . I never wanted 'im to go fishin'. 'Cause when we lived out there on the islands, I never got any school. I got dear little bit. An' then I didn't have anybody to show me anyt'ing . . . an' I had to go to work. You had no choice. I learnt a little my own self, that I did. I learnt to read a little, figure a little bit. Not very much. Figure a little bit – keep somebody from cheatin' me. I'm only foolin' about that!

I tried to get a teacher . . . out home in the house for to teach Ernest. An' I was after one . . . I knowed she was pretty good. I didn't make no success at that. You would have to pay so much. An' I know what I felt like . . . I liked for him to get an education. An' that's what my plans was. I didn't want 'im to go fishin'.

Well, we moved off o' the island. "Now," I t'ought to myself, " now you can get your education." An' he got up to grade eight . . . but he took no more interest in goin' to school than . . . He was fish, fish, an' work. Wherever he could get around the water an' boats – that's what he wanted to do. That's all he wanted to do. Well, I come home one day. Anne said, "Ernest's all t'rough school." I . . . I don't know what I said. But I didn't feel very good.

Then I says, "He's all t'rough?"

"Yes. He's all t'rough." You know it made me feel some bad. It made me . . . really I did feel bad because I didn't have any amount o' money but I planned to give him some education. When he was t'rough here he would go somewheres else that he'd get an education. That was my plan. If he didn't use it, it was no load to carry. If he wanted it any time, he had it. But all fishin', fishin'. An' I told 'im so many times I didn't want 'im to go fishin'. But he's still fishin'. How many years he can keep at it I can't tell you. He'll go I guess till there ain't no fish. An' by God, that time don't seem to be so far off. The way it's goin' . . . if there's no fish to get, what will he do? But like the feller said, it's no good to holler – complainin' don't do no good.

When I first stayed home from vessel fishin', Theodore was a baby . . . about t'ree months old. An' I was lobsterin' then. An' I marked a trap for 'im – marked the buoy, you know. An' whatever I got then – out o' that trap – a couple o' cents maybe – was for 'im, you. So I set seventeen traps at Black Rock one day, an' I had his trap wit'. An' the next mornin', I went out to haul an' I hauled along, an' come to his trap. An' it had this nice big lobster into it. I took his lobster an' I put it separate, up in the boat house, up in the bow.

On the way home Jake Mosher met me – he'd buy an' sell lobsters, you understand. Well, Jake waved to me to stop. I stopped, an' Jake said, "You got any lobsters to sell?"

"Yes Jake," I said. "I got a couple. I might as well sell 'em."

An' I sold 'em to Jake, an' when I had my couple weighed out, I reached in the boat house up for'ard an' got this one I had for Theodore. An' I put that in the basket an' it weighed exact four pounds. An' Jakey opened up his whole money kettle, you, an' hauled me out a dollar bill, passed me a dollar – twenty-five cents a pound. Well, that went to my son. Most all o' the fellers around, if they've got a child, they marked a trap for 'im . . . an' you give that child every cent that you made into it. It seems a trap for your child beats you . . . your other traps all to pieces – always more lobsters into that than any of the others, you. I seen that happen time an' time again.

Anyways, when Theodore got a little older he come wit' me – went out wit' me fishin'. But he's growed up now . . . works in Dartmouth, there in the hospital – thirteen years altoget'er. An' he still has this in his mind – to get home . . . home so he could get an old boat. T'ree winters ago he said, "I'm goin' to make up traps." I helped him. An' here lays everyt'in' yet . . . the bows is all bent into the sills. I knit all the headin's for 'im . . . an' everyt'in'. An' it all lays there in the store . . . . An' every once in a while he comes down. He says, "I got a notion to make a set." Two years he's been sayin' that. Fishin' is still in his mind . . . it's hard to get clear of it . . . once it's in your blood.

The younger fellers are leavin' fishin' 'cause it's gettin' harder to make a livin' at it an' the cost o' gear today the way it is it just costs too much to fit up. They'd better go . . . an' work somewheres an' not get into it. That's the way it looks to me. Our hours is so bad. Take from four o'clock in the mornin' till . . . it can be till nine, ten o'clock at night. An' you can go anywheres in a factory today an' work eight hours an' be done wit' it. Five o'clock comes, you're done. I wouldn't tell any o' my boys to go fishin' because I t'ink there's easier work to get an' I t'ink they could make more money at just about anyt'ing.

See, the way it's goin' now, I'll tell you . . . it's goin' backwards. At one time there was fish to catch. If I had the gear then, like I got now, I could o' made a dollar. But I didn't have it. Now I got the gear to work wit' an' well . . . now it's no good to me because there's not'in' there to catch. So you're lost. That's the way I see it.

Years ago when I fished wit' Dad, I helped him dress herrin' for ten cents an hour. That's what I got . . . ten cents an hour. My father would give me a few dollars at the end o' the week . . . I earned that in the boat fishin' wit' 'im. An' after a while I started to get a little gear of my own. The first nets I had I was around twelve years old. I bought two . . . paid six dollars apiece for 'em. Well, after I got the two nets an' got some herrin' into 'em . . . I'd get a few dollars for 'em. An' when I'd get a few dollars I'd buy anot'er net. An' the first lobster trap I ever had, I picked up laths from smashed traps around the shore an' made it. The first boat I ever had was only an old t'ing that somebody else wouldn't use.

An' for a young feller to fit out today . . . look at the price o' boats. What do they want for 'em? Up to the west'ard, from four I t'ink, or four hundred an' fifty a foot. An' that's just the hull . . . no engine. The first boat I had cost me five hundred dollars. An' the new one . . . eight t'ousand dollars. An' now if you was to go to buy a new one . . . fifteen, twenty t'ousand. If you wanted a hundred lobster traps I would say o'er a t'ousand dollars. An' if you wanted twenty nets . . . you should have twenty on account o' some gettin' tore to pieces – a net'd cost fifty dollars. An' you need grapplin's, buoys, rope . . . it'd cost you thirty or forty t'ousand to fit out . . . just to start. Just to make a start at it. An' you're goin' to do a lot o' work to get any o' that money back. The way fishin' is now . . . why a young feller'd be some foolish to fit out. He'd never get his money back . . . be in debt as long as he lives.

It's really . . . it's a lot o' downfalls, it really is. You're gettin' very little at it for the time an' work. I could quite easy give it up an' work ashore. Not that I want to be a millionaire or anyt'in', but there's really no money into it. There just ain't no fish around like there was one time. An' by the time you get your expenses off, you haven't got too much left as far as . . . for your profit. You really haven't. Look at your nets – there's so many t'ings – the dogfish an' the sharks. These past few summers the blue sharks was some desperate . . . right t'ick, you, around the nets. Tearin' the nets to pieces. You set a bunch o' nets out there . . . they would have 'em ruined as fast as you put 'em out. Well, you don't get what fish you could get an' then you got to set in the store half o' the winter an' mend those nets . . . mend day in an' day out. Same t'ing . . . you may set your lobster traps off in the fall o' the year – maybe you set two hundred or two hundred an' fifty traps. Y'know, you're lucky to get a few hauls in an' get a few lobsters before you lose your traps. An' you can just about count on losin' a good part o' your traps. I set out a bunch o' traps two seasons ago – a hundred an' seventy-five or eighty – an' it come a storm. I set one day an' I never got the first haul in. It smashed the works up that night. It don't take long. An' you got them to replace. An' the cost o' gear today . . . why, I guess a feller'd get discouraged even if he was makin' a dollar.

There is times I'd'a liked to had a lot of education . . . maybe I could o' got a better job. But now it wouldn't matter how much I had – I don't t'ink it would make any difference because I'm at the age . . . I heard come over television – the feller he was so mad. He said when you get in your forties . . . why you're past forty they say, "You're no good, we don't want you." I t'ink that's terrible. Because I really know fellers that's forty, fifty an' so on, is smarter an' can do more than what the younger fellers can do right today. An' I'm not foolin'. I don't know why they t'ink you can't do nothin'.

But I guess you go along wit' it as best you can. You take each day as it comes. You take a feller like me that's been in fishin' now for a quantity o' years . . . there's not too much else you can go an' do. As for me goin' somewheres now an' gettin' into a plant . . . like I said, you can't get in. A younger feller has more of a show – he's got more education, he's young an' he's got . . . they got a chance. But you take right along the South Shore here, most o' the majority o' the fellers are middle aged men . . . they can't just go everywhere an' get a job.

Gregory – he's only seven now – he's got it in his mind to be a fisherman. But till the time he gets ready to go fishin' . . . I'll tell you the truth, till he goes fishin', it'll just be anot'er . . . it'll be anot'er past. I can't see how it's goin' to hold up 'cause there just ain't no fish out there. They're slackin' off every summer. So I say there's no future for a young person today. I wouldn't want anybody to start fishin' any more . . . an' I hope Gregory forgets about it. I mean . . . it's a hard t'ing to say . . . you just can't . . . Might be wrong an' I hope I am, but I really believe there's no way. The small fellers are goin' to have to get out of it 'cause you can't make enough to buy the gear. It don't look good. No sir.

Listen, I'm fifty-four years old. I've never seen a vacation since I was a kid. In fifty-four years. That's all right, ain't it? I t'ink a feller's foolish. It's just foolishness for anybody to go fishin' today. My son was never too anxious about goin' fishin' an' I never encouraged 'im on it 'cause to me . . . look, any job you can make twice as much as what you can make at this job. An' so much easier. At this job you don't know if you're makin' five cents or five dollars. It's just a gamble . . . a losin' game, you. I told my young feller, I said, "Look, if you got the brains, learn. Don't stop. Keep on. 'Cause as far as goin' out there, I ain't fussy if you go out. I don't want you to do what I done."

So now he's got a pretty good job. He's up there in the Michelin plant. He's got a pretty good job. I don't begrudge it to him one bit. But years ago, these old fellers, they t'ought what they done, the other feller had to do. An' that was it. I can't see that point myself. Listen, if you can go to a plant today an' make a day's work . . . why should you go off here in a boat day after day pullin' yourself to pieces?

If the whole t'ing changes in the next twenty-five years as it did in this twenty-five, why I don't know how you're goin' to survive. I don't know what my three boys are growin' up into an' I'd hate to be them when they get my age 'cause I don't know how they'll keep the t'ing goin'. I'm afraid someday that it's goin' to be a big change . . . for the worse. What I'm tellin' you, times has changed – good an' well changed too. Everyt'in' is goin' too fast. The future ain't good . . . I don't know what's goin' to happen.

# Acknowledgements

My gratitude is extended to J. Lynton Martin, Director of the Nova Scotia Museum, and to Mary Sparling, Director of the Art Gallery at Mount Saint Vincent University in Halifax, who were instrumental in the organization and national circulation of "Images of Lunenburg County," an exhibit of text and photographs which included material selected from this book.

I would especially like to thank the men of Lunenburg County and their families who so generously shared part of their lives with me. The personal experience that lies behind this book is one of friendship and respect for people like Sydney Tanner. Their warmth and kindness will remain with me.

*P.B.*